CAR BADGES

The ultimate guide to automotive logos worldwide

CAR
BADGES

The ultimate guide to automotive logos worldwide

GILES CHAPMAN

MERRELL
LONDON · NEW YORK

CONTENTS

INTRODUCTION

Car books generally slake the thirst of the fanatic with statistics and specification, or else daze the casual reader with jargon about design, engineering or motor sport. Reading this one, however, you'll end up better acquainted with the serif than the supercharger, more familiar with heraldry than hot-rodding. You will find within the text the background to just about every car badge, logo or emblem you're likely to encounter on this planet's roads, and quite a few more that you might only glimpse on the museum pieces of the motoring world. Do not expect to delight (or drown) in the usual automotive data: what you are about to read are the true stories behind the trademarks affixed to the cars we all know, and more often than not they revolve around ego, enterprise and ambition.

Many of these trademarks, coincidentally, are also extremely attractive, and their origins may well have been puzzling you for years. That's why *Car Badges* is the size it is. If you wish, you can keep this book in your car's glove box and, the next time you're sitting in traffic (and aren't you always?), you can fish it out, and the logo on the car in front will no longer be a graphic mystery.

In the rollercoaster history of vehicle identity, the car badge is currently enjoying one of its golden periods. Or, rather, silver periods. With manufacturing and marketing power concentrated in the hands of just ten multinational groups, plus a handful of independents and outcasts, product differentiation has never been so important. Badges are one extremely cost-effective way of using cars as rolling billboards, and Volkswagen, Citroën and Honda are taking maximum advantage of this opportunity, increasing the size of their emblems to previously unseen proportions so that the passer-by is left in no doubt as to whose model he or she has just clocked.

At the same time, however, there is a striking similarity between many of today's car badges. They're mostly finished in gleaming, chrome-effect plastic, most often broadly circular in form or frame, and in a large number of cases they adopt stylized alphabet characters. Give a manufacturer a completely clean sheet of paper and it will still produce something that it considers to be 'distinctive' yet that is, in reality, totally generic – Infiniti being a prime example.

The car badge today seeks to inform but is anxious not to offend, which is probably why gold, with its is-it/isn't-it in fashion dilemma, is rarely used, why the few colours that are used in badge design are generally sober, and why the human visage seems to be an absolute no-no; even animal forms tend to avoid eye contact, with the combative exception of Jaguar.

It is difficult to blame today's automotive executives for badge blandness; they've been following one another ever since the car was invented. In the pioneer days of the 1890s, motor cars were the work of serious-minded

After the British Motor Corporation hoisted its banner over Austin, Morris, Wolseley, Riley and MG in 1952, the fate of all five brands was sealed as the new era of mass 'badge engineering' dawned; only MG has just about survived.

engineers who seemed, from today's perspective, blissfully unconcerned about what we would now call marketing. Messrs Benz, Levassor and Lanchester wanted potential buyers to admire their work in cracking the problem of internal combustion and its handy by-product of self-propelled transport. Impressing customers with packaging was something they considered more appropriate for biscuit tins.

However, the branding of motor cars soon became important as dozens of 'me-too' products mushroomed in the USA and western Europe. Car design wasn't rocket science for very long. One of the first mass-produced cars, the 1901 Oldsmobile 'Curved Dash' model, displayed an elaborate emblem on its side panels, but most manufacturers chose a car's mesh grille protecting the front-mounted radiator – its 'face' – as the best place to display their trademarks. From the early years of the twentieth century until just before the First World War, this trademark

Ford's blue 'script-in-oval' is one of the most familiar car badges anywhere on the planet, so it's strange to think that for over thirty-five years, between 1939 and 1976, it was absent from Ford cars – models such as this Mustang tended to have individual liveries and plain F-O-R-D letter identification.

usually took the form of a script in the curly, Art Nouveau-influenced style of the day as a skeletal brass stamping; after the War most manufacturers plumped for a centre spot on the front of the metal cowling surrounding the radiator itself for emblem-like badges, into which they began to pour genuine creative effort. At first these were also made of brass, but intricately coloured enamel soon followed.

Rolls-Royce is not usually considered a pioneer of marketing techniques but, in car badge terms, it was a trailblazer. Its elegant badge first appeared in 1906 as part of an impressively built and presented package. There is plenty of evidence to suggest that Rolls-Royce didn't necessarily make the "best car in the world", but its distinguished badge definitely played a part in extracting this accolade from a journalist at The Times in 1908.

The car logo/emblem phenomenon of the 1920s and 1930s was without doubt the wing. This essential apparatus of any bird was attached to dozens of badges to

heighten the image of potential speed in those days before speed limits and road deaths were of any concern. Sometimes, as for Hispano-Suiza, the wings were apposite; sometimes, as for Hillman, they were a rather desperate attempt to sprinkle a boring brand with a sheen of charisma. They generally survive today on cars in which sporting prowess has actually been proven as part of a rich heritage.

Rolls-Royce led the way in innovation yet again in 1946 when it invented the concept of 'badge engineering'. This was the practice – a natural step on the road towards economies of scale – of selling exactly the same car with different badges, as evinced by Rolls-Royce's Silver Dawn and the Bentley MkVI. In Britain more than anywhere else, this practice became a ruse to keep a bewildering range of brands alive at a fraction of the cost of giving them individually designed models; it reached its peak in 1965 when the British Motor Corporation (BMC) could

offer the same car (which had been designed under the codename ADO 16) as an Austin, a Morris, a Riley, a Wolseley, an MG and a Vanden Plas; these six venerable badges had never had to work so hard.

Badge engineering was ultimately counter-productive. There was plenty of choice but little competition and, in the case of such organizations as BMC and the Rootes Group, all their brands so treated tended to go into slow but terminal decline simultaneously. A more successful trend came from designers working in Detroit in the late 1940s and early 1950s. Such models as the 1953 Corvette and 1954 Thunderbird came with such a strong image to match their sexy styling that they quickly became sub-brands in their own right. This development led to a move away from a strong marque identity towards unique decoration and insignia for each product line, with such famous design chiefs as Virgil Exner and Harley Earl consigning emblem designs,

Badge modesty is a thing of the past: in the twenty-first century, they are getting bigger and bolder, and these two Hondas – a 1983 Accord saloon on the left and a 2005 CR-V off-roader – demonstrate how the badge has become, over twenty years, a prominent design centrepiece on the typical modern car.

sometimes dating back fifty years, to the dustbin of history. Nascent motor industries, such as Japan's, naturally aped this approach, with such early models as Crowns and Bluebirds barely identifiable as the respective Toyotas and Datsuns they were.

Today it seems amazing to consider that between 1939 and 1976 Ford's 'blue oval' did not feature on any of its products, or that Chevrolet's 'bow tie' had all but vanished from its cars in the 1980s. But the 1960s and 1970s saw branding become a big issue, and a clean-up operation got under way that was to see car manufacturers' trademarks and the identity of their products become inseparable. Companies often had corporate logos that were at odds with the badges on their cars, or even a marketing brand completely different from the manufacturer's name, which resulted in an inconsistency that reflected poorly as the industry consolidated. Once again, Britain was a prime culprit, with the name

of a truck company (Leyland) imposed on cars that had strong brand identities of their own. There was also the bizarre situation of Nissan actually selling Datsuns and American Motors marketing the unpopular Rambler. All of these developments created confusion and ended in hasty changes that only upset the delicate equilibrium of customer confidence.

And so we come to modern times. The saga of the car badge continues, with those that have lost their lustre – Oldsmobile, Plymouth, Jensen – quickly forgotten, and newcomers – Smart, Perodua, Tata – becoming familiar seemingly overnight. We could also be on the verge of a new car brand onslaught from China, as the country's one hundred-plus car firms compete for ultimate survival. Western car makers simply want to colonize this massive potential market with their own brands, but the Chinese government knows that the trick to long-term success is in intellectual property

rights. This book focuses on Geely and ZhongHua as potentially massive all-Chinese brands of the future; they have already taken the trouble to create logos for their cars that could one day be familiar on roads worldwide, as identifiably Chinese as Ferrari's prancing horse is Italian and Mercedes-Benz's three-pointed star is German.

There have been around seven thousand marques worldwide since Carl Benz built the first motor car in 1885. This book studies 125 badges. It includes every significant car badge currently in production, plus others that are famous, intriguing, beautiful or even scandalous. The text brings together many facts and stories for the first time in one publication; it aims to describe not only 'what' but also 'why'. Words in single quotation marks are expressed exactly as they appear on the badge or logo in question. For example, 'PORSCHE' is printed in capital letters if capital letters appear on the badge. Similarly, 'Pierce' is initially printed in upper

An interesting example of badges being used to leverage economies of scale is this line-up of people-carriers launched in 1994; made by the SEVEL joint venture between Fiat and Peugeot, it is principally the use of different badges that allows the same car to become a Citroën, a Fiat, a Peugeot or a Lancia.

and lower case but later appears as 'PIERCE ARROW' in order to reflect a real-life change on the badge itself.

As a rule, however, this book avoids the jargons of typography, heraldry and the colour palette. For example, the text uses the word 'purple' to describe a colour even if a precise Pantone reference for the particular intensity of magenta might have been obtainable. Using the technical term 'serif', however, is unavoidable. Perhaps the best description of the term is found in Simon Loxley's fascinating *Type: The Secret History of Letters*: "the little 'tab' at the end of strokes". A sans serif letter ('*sans*' is the French word for 'without') is one that does not have serifs.

A final consideration is whether car badges really matter or not. A car is one of the most complex, multi-functioning consumer items it is possible to buy. However, the size, location, nuance and message conveyed by a car's badge has little bearing on the machine's characteristics or abilities; it's a finishing touch rather than a defining facet. But badges emit a strange power that can put enthusiasts under a spell. The right badge helps sell cars, as a survey of used car prices recently conducted in the UK revealed. The Lotus Elise and Vauxhall 220 are sports cars that are pretty similar except for the detail of their body shapes and badges. They are built on the same production line at Lotus's factory in Norwich, England, and retailed for around the same price (£23,160 for the Lotus, against £22,980 for the Vauxhall) in 2001. However, after three years the Lotus had merely drifted down in value to £17,685, while the Vauxhall had plummeted to £12,990. The difference, £4695, would easily pay for another decent used car.

Apply these figures to the wider world – a Mercedes-Benz versus an Opel in Germany, a BMW taking on a Lincoln in the US, maybe soon even a ZhongHua battling a Geely in China – and the tangible importance of badges, and the brand values they convey, is all too apparent. On the basest level, as much as for fascinating insights into a car company's background, culture and ethos, the evidence suggests that they matter a lot.

CAR BADGES A–Z

ABARTH

If ever a badge summed up what a car was all about, then it is the vivid trademark adopted by Carlo Abarth in 1949. His sports-racing cars were small but extremely effective, just like the scorpion depicted in the badge (he was also born under the Scorpio star sign), and from 1956 they really did have a sting in their tails too, after Abarth turned his engine-tuning magic wand towards the rear-engined Fiat 600 and sprinkled it with high-performance gold dust. This, alongside hotted-up versions of the later Nuova 500 and 850, introduced a generation of young European drivers to motor sport in the era before the Mini Cooper lured them away.

Born Karl Abarth in 1908 in Vienna, the former motorcycle racer and engineering entrepreneur needed a strong brand. Designing and building a huge assortment of sporting cars between 1949 and 1971 – an activity that barely broke even – Abarth nevertheless stayed in business through selling Abarth-tagged performance accessories for Fiats and Simcas, especially exhaust systems.

So the Abarth badge, a shield with a bold diagonal colour split between red and yellow, and the curled-up scorpion set menacingly in the centre, is used on many more cars than the few thousand special models that left Abarth's Turin workshops. It often appeared as nothing more than a large sticker, and on some prototypes, just as a white, stylized outline of the gruesome creature alone.

Fiat took over in 1971, and it was the power of the Abarth badge more than Carlo Abarth's methodology that came to the fore. It was attached to high-performance versions of the Fiat 131, Ritmo/Strada, Uno and, today, the Seicento and Panda. It still bears the legend 'ABARTH & C.' arched across the top, but the historical nuance is weakening by the year for a generation of speed freaks who have grown up with the Subaru Impreza Turbo and BMW M3 as 'heroes'.

AC

Founded in 1901, AC is the oldest surviving independent British motor manufacturer; the company maintains its reputation for handbuilt excellence with a factory in Surrey, England, where craftsmen still hand-beat aluminium bodies for the legendary Cobra sports car.

The hallowed initials stand for Auto Carriers, a partnership between an engineer and a wealthy butcher; Auto Carriers Ltd made a kind of three-wheeled delivery vehicle with a single-cylinder air-cooled engine. In 1907 it devised a passenger-carrying edition called the Sociable, and a few years later the company was doing a roaring trade in handsome, high-quality sports cars. For which the name Auto Carriers, of course, was wholly inappropriate. But the acronym stuck, and the catchy initials were artfully curved and stylized into a circle that could be forged on to the ends of the cars' wheel hubs.

It also made a neat badge and, although the surrounding circle was added from about 1925 to more successfully hold the initials together, it's remained on the front of every AC since. Thanks to its graphic simplicity, most incarnations have been faithful to the original. One of the stranger applications of the AC badge was on the front of a three-wheeled invalid car that the company produced for the UK's National Health Service in the 1960s. However, you will search for the badge in vain on most genuine Cobras, because the Cobra has always been sold as a Shelby in the USA, its biggest market. Only a tiny number of the lightweight Ford V8-powered two-seaters are distributed elsewhere with an AC badge.

ACURA

Acura is largely unknown outside North America, to which markets it is exclusively dedicated. It is, officially, "the performance luxury division of the American Honda Motor Company" (together with its Canadian and Mexican counterparts) and, as it was launched in 1986, Acura predates its Lexus counterpart by three years.

Its logo, looking rather like an arrowhead framed in a chunky ellipse, strongly suggests an 'A' with its two elongated diamond stems and tiny crossbar. It also resembles a pair of compasses used in geometry, which unconsciously suggests the image of engineering precision. It is fitted to Acura cars in chrome outline, and appears on communications in black silhouette with a block-letter 'ACURA' beneath.

Unlike Lexus, Acura has always marketed existing Honda designs that have been rebranded for US consumption, to distance them from Honda's more humble family car fare (such as the

Accord, which for many years was the top-selling passenger car in the USA). The first models were Acura editions of the Honda Legend and Integra, and in 1990 they were joined by the Acura NSX mid-engined supercar, sold elsewhere as a Honda.

The sales success of the early Acura Legend is due in large part to the fact that it offered luxury based on qualities rarely found in luxury cars of the day, such as precise handling and responsive powertrains – in stark contrast to the wallowing giants offered by the Detroit 'establishment'. Honda's Acura nameplate has steadily migrated to other car market sectors, in particular the sport-utility vehicle one with the Acura MDX in 2000; this was conceived and developed at Honda's R&D centre in Ohio, and subsequently built in the USA. The all-new 2005 Acura RL luxury saloon is the first car sold in the country to feature a telematics system with 'real-time' traffic information updated twenty-four hours a day in several metropolitan areas.

ALFA ROMEO

The first ALFA car of 1910 (left) bore the Milanese coat of arms that has remained familiar ever since, even after the company was acquired by Nicola Romeo in 1915 and changed its name. Below: the V-shaped prow of a 1920s model permitted the fitting of a badge on each facet of the radiator shell for easy identification. Opposite: exquisite detailing of the badge setting for this Alfa Romeo sports car of the 1930s.

When Anonima Lombarda Fabbrica Automobili (ALFA, and equating to the Lombardy Car Factory Ltd) was founded in 1910, the company's management immediately created a logo by combining two familiar symbols of the city of Milan. The red cross was part of the city's coat of arms, and the serpent was a heraldic icon used by the aristocratic Visconti family. These were two elements that, in tradition and meaning, were far removed, but that together signified the marque's locality and invincible power.

The cross is reminiscent of the symbol carried by the Lombard battalion that embarked on the First Crusade in 1095. At the head of this army marching to the Holy Land was Ottone Visconti, master of Invorio and Oleggio Castello, and an ancestor of the Visconti family who three hundred years later ruled Milan. When the Lombard battalion returned to Milan in 1100, the city adopted the cross motif as its municipal coat of arms in recognition of the bravery shown by its knights in their battle for the holy cause.

The story behind the serpent is more curious. It dates back to the sixth century when the Germanic Lombard tribes invaded and then settled in northern Italy. They believed a serpent on a blue background brought good luck, and used the symbol on their battle flags. When Matteo Visconti became lord of Milan in 1295 he asked his more learned courtiers to invent a Visconti history for him that would ennoble a somewhat inglorious past. They selected an association with the Lombard settlers, and so the serpent became the emblem of the Visconti coat of arms. To reinforce this imaginary link between the Visconti clan and the ancient Germanic people, a new myth was concocted whereby a Lombard, Matteo's ancestor Umberto, had rid the surrounding countryside of a terrible dragon. So the court's heraldic designers created the 'biscione', which had the body of the Lombard snake and a dragon's head.

The original shield-style badge, used

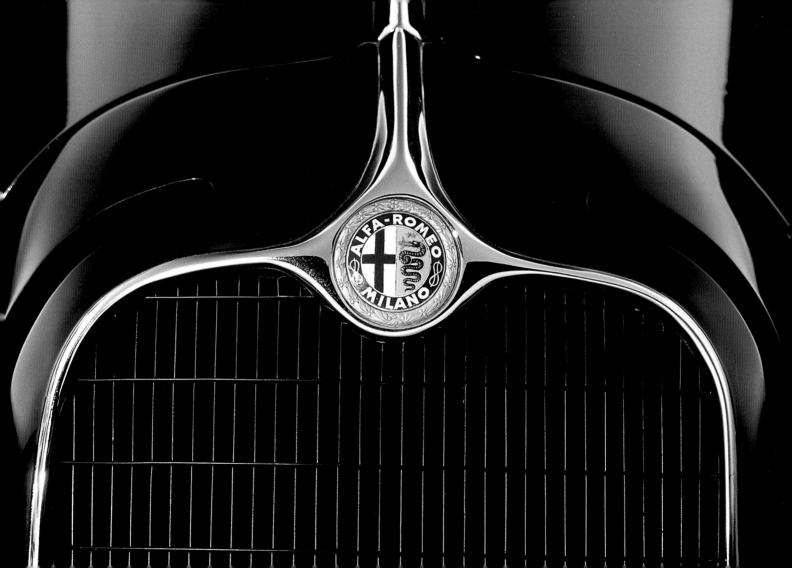

Left, from left to right: subtle evolution of the Alfa Romeo badge saw its most radical change in 1971, when the word 'MILANO' was dropped. Below: grille and badge detailing has always been artfully executed.

by ALFA between 1910 and 1915, was circular and divided in two: the left side bore the red cross on a white background, while on the right the imaginary Visconti serpent was shown devouring a human enemy. A Savoy knot motif was used to separate the two words 'ALFA' and 'MILANO' around the edge. It was modified in 1913 when the brass letters became white, more pronounced and outlined in gold. In addition, the double Savoy knot was made more robust and the serpent depiction simplified.

Two years later, Nicola Romeo took over the company and in 1918 the word 'ALFA' was replaced by the words 'ALFA-ROMEO'. The logo remained unchanged until 1925 when, after winning the first Grand Prix world championship, a silver-coloured laurel wreath running around the whole circumference was added; the colour of the outlines around the letters and knots also changed to silver. Anomalously, in 1932 the badge on cars for export to France bore the words 'ALFA-ROMEO PARIS'.

In 1946 Italy became a republic and so the Savoy knots – suggestive of the royal family that had previously ruled the country – were replaced on the circular shield by wavy lines.

Certain models during the years 1946–50 have a revised logo with letters and symbols in relief on a red background, but it wasn't until 1971, when Alfa Romeo's new plant for Alfasud production in Naples was inaugurated, that the last change was made. The style of the logo was modernized: the serpent symbol, still with its victim half-way down its throat, became much simpler and the hyphen between 'ALFA' and 'ROMEO' disappeared. With the company expanding in southern Italy, it also seemed like a good time to drop the word 'MILANO'.

The shield-shaped grille has long been a key design element of Alfa Romeo's sporty cars, including the GT 1300 Junior of the late 1960s (below) and the 147 of today (right).

288 PA

Take a test drive for two
(You and your ego)

ST02 FSY

ALLARD

Classic Allards such as this J2 (opposite) featured the simple 'ALLARD' badge, while later cars such as the Safari estate (below) incorporated a giant 'A' in the nose design. A stillborn 1991 revival (below) came with this evocative logo.

Sydney Allard remains to this day the only man to win an international rally in a car that he designed and built. In 1952 Allard, from south London, slid his way to victory in the Monte Carlo Rally, driving an Allard P1 saloon. If King George VI hadn't died at the same time, Allard would have been hailed a sporting hero on every newspaper's front page.

Just as remarkable was Sydney Allard's rise to car manufacturer status. It began with a home-built sports car that scored spectacular wins in off-road trials in the 1930s thanks to low weight and Ford V8 power. Friends asked for replicas, and in 1946 Allard launched a proper production car, the J1, with sidevalve V8 Ford engine and ugly, if charismatic, looks.

They were brutes to handle, super-powerful, and formidable in motor sport, with the later J2 and J2X putting up a good show at such races as Le Mans. Although fewer than two thousand cars were made sporadically over a fourteen-year period until 1960, it was a mighty

achievement. Allards were constructed in a labyrinth of workshops in south London, often using materials salvaged from war-time scrap yards and engines mysteriously procured when imports were hard to get. The unstoppable rise of Jaguar – and the cars' increasingly antique nature – finished the marque off.

The Allard badge was as simple and rugged as the cars themselves, the 'ALLARD' word in utilitarian, three-dimensional capitals on a black enamel background, framed in a curvy rectangle. It looks like the badge on the front of an Aga cooker – highly appropriate in view of Allard cars' cast-iron longevity.

The M2X, P2 and Safari estate models also sported a radiator grille shaped like a giant capital 'A', so there was no mistaking them thundering down the road. An attempt to revive Allard in 1991 introduced a new logo, with the crossbar of the 'A' curving upwards to meet the upper serif of the 'd', but both car and logo vanished very soon afterwards.

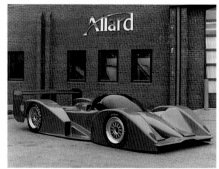

ALPINE

Opposite: the Alpine
badge was made more
obviously 'French' for an
attack on the US market
with the A610 that never
happened; below: an
Alpine A110 (left) and an
A310 showing the
circular badge just
above the rear wheel.

Jean Rédélé does not loom large in the motor industry Hall of Fame, yet in 1955 he founded Alpine, the most successful brand of French sports car ever. Not that it was much cherished: Renault quietly abandoned Alpine in 1995 after forty years.

Rédélé, a Dieppe-based Renault dealer and amateur racing driver, chose the name Alpine after his victory in the Coupe des Alpes (Alpine Rally) in 1953. The distinctive Alpine badge, a twin-ringed circle with a leaning capital 'A' in the centre, with a crossbar that resembled a Nike-like 'swoosh' arrow to denote speed, first appeared on the A106. This had a sporty, streamlined plastic body on a Renault 4CV chassis, and from this, a long series of rear-engined sports cars including the A108, A110 Berlinette, A310, GTA and A610 were made.

Alpines competed at Le Mans for the first time in 1963. The cars were always competition-orientated – hence the keynote colour of the badge being the mid-blue long used as France's national racing colour. There was never an outright victory but plenty of class wins. In 1971 Renault contracted all its racing activities to Alpine, and went on to win at Le Mans in 1978.

The fuel crisis of the 1970s saw Renault absorb Alpine entirely. In 1991, Renault decided to polish Alpine's image prior to launching the GTA on the lucrative US market. Part of this campaign was a new badge. The circle was replaced by a wide silver oval carrying the 'ALPINE' lettering in white and two swatches of red, white and blue stripes to emphasize the car's French origins. The capital 'A' also came in for attention, slimmed down but given a drop-shadow for a more three-dimensional effect.

But then the US debut was cancelled and the last Alpine was made in 1995, to the sadness of loyal enthusiasts.

ALVIS

Today Alvis is one of the UK's leading defence companies, making all manner of battlefield vehicles designed to withstand and then annihilate anything an enemy force can muster. In this sphere, an attractive logo is the last thing on anyone's mind. But Alvis has one, and it's rooted in the company's inauguration in 1919 as a car manufacturer.

The word Alvis is derived from the name of a component maker, Aluminium Alloy Pistons Ltd. Geoffrey de Freville, the founder, used 'Alvis' as the trademark for a piston, and then designed an entire engine. He thought the name sounded good in any language. A Welsh engineer, T.G. John, considered it an excellent power unit, and put it in the first Alvis car in 1920.

The original Alvis piston carried a simple trademark of the 'ALVIS' name in a red triangle, with the letter 'V' most prominent and the others in diminishing size either side towards the acute corners of the shape. For the first car's radiator badge, the Alvis founders turned the emblem on its head, and added flowing wings either side and dark-blue and green enamel in the background. Legal action swiftly followed when the AVRO aircraft company accused Alvis of infringing its own badge; AVRO were successful, so by 1922 Alvis had reverted to red, a downward-pointing tip, and an additional band above the 'ALVIS' word in white for a fuller frame effect.

Alvis cars were innovative in the 1920s, introducing front-wheel drive, and in the 1930s were powerful sports tourers with stylish coachwork. After the Second World War, Alvises were quality luxury cars, sportier than a Daimler but cheaper than a Bentley. Throughout this entire period, the Alvis badge endured on each model, cast in brass, then chromed and coloured with red enamel. The only difference was in the curvature of the casting, to match the profile of each model's radiator shell.

From 1945 onwards, however, cars were a sideline, as Alvis's defence division saw massive growth. Ironically, John had diversified into aero engines as early as 1935, but only to finance car making. Rover bought the company in 1965, and the last Alvis car was built two years later. Although Alvis then became part of British Leyland, a buyout in 1981 saved the day. Happily, the red Alvis triangle is still the firm's corporate logo, and some tanks also bear the venerable trademark as a large aluminium casting. Surviving cars are catered for by a company, appropriately called Red Triangle, which took on the Alvis spares inventory and records.

AMERICAN MOTORS

Opposite and below:
the Pacer is AMC's most
famous, some would say
notorious, product;
bottom: the weirdly
named Gremlin model
carried this distinctive,
impish emblem.

American Motors was a car brand that happened by degrees. The American Motors Corporation was formed in 1954 when two old-established marques, Hudson and Nash, merged their operations to compete better with General Motors and Ford. In 1957 the old-fashioned names were ditched and all the cars carried the Rambler badge. This strategy persisted for another ten years, during which Ramblers consistently failed to lure customers away from Chevrolet, Plymouth and Ford. It was time for another rethink.

This time, the Wisconsin-based company decided to apply its corporate name to its cars. At the same time, the old American Motors logo, a straightforward if dated pairing of a streamlined 'A' and 'M' in a two-tone square, was made redundant. A new version was created by New York corporate identity specialists Lippincott & Margulies – a clean, fresh design featuring a red, white and blue rectangle with the simplest possible suggestion of a capital letter 'A'. 'American Motors' featured below

in bold roman type, and the whole thing was always meant to be on a white background.

Customers were now expected to refer to their Gremlins, Hornets, Rebels and Ambassadors as 'American Motors' cars, but the natural shorthand of AMC proved such welcome relief from this cumbersome title that, from the 1976 season and the launch of the woeful Pacer 'economy' car, the cars were officially called AMCs.

The timelessness of the Lippincott & Margulies badge, often seen on cars as a simple chrome addition, meant that it saw American Motors through to 1987, when it was acquired by Chrysler for $600 million, principally for its under-developed Jeep division. Almost the first thing the new owner did was scrap AMC.

ASTON MARTIN

Lionel Martin and Robert Bamford began their partnership in a London garage, the success of which gave birth to the idea of building their very own sports car in 1921. Martin had competed successfully in the punishing hill-climb at Aston Clinton in Buckinghamshire, and it was from this event that the compound name for their new car originated.

The original Aston Martin badge, created in 1920, took the form of a circle in which the letters 'A' and 'M' were placed, overlapping one another in a classical monogram. Finished in dark-green enamel on a brass background, it is thought to have been the work of the wealthy Lionel Martin's wife, Kate. This Aston Martin badge was the first of several, each reflecting a different stage in the marque's history.

By 1930, when Aston Martin had garnered an excellent reputation on road and track, a 'winged' theme had been adopted: a bird-like image of feathered wings on which the 'ASTON MARTIN' legend

was carved. The arms of the prominent, central capital 'M' rose up and flowed back and upwards over the two words, incorporating the horizontal strokes of both 'T's.

A less elaborate rendition soon followed, but in 1932 it was redesigned by S.C.H. 'Sammy' Davis, famous in his earlier days as one of Bentley's race team drivers and latterly a leading writer with Britain's magazine *The Autocar*. Davis had a fascination with Egyptology, taking as his inspiration for the revised, open-winged shape the scarab beetle in flight. The badge was finished in silver gilt for the outline and 'ribs', with cream enamel as an infill. Framed centrally within the wings, in a rectangle, the name Aston Martin was set in silver letters on a black enamel background. It suggested speed and class neatly rolled into one.

A celebrity badge designer was one thing; a new company owner was quite another. When industrialist David Brown bought Aston Martin in 1947, a slightly

Three classics from Aston Martin's illustrious past; right: a 1934 Le Mans model; below, left: a 2-litre tourer of the mid-1930s; below, right: a DB2.

revised badge now stacked 'DAVID BROWN' symmetrically above 'ASTON MARTIN' in an obvious graphic ego trip. That's how it stayed until he sold the company in 1972, although the base colour changed from chrome to gold in 1971.

Since then, the design has twice been tweaked to keep it contemporary. In 1984 the ends of each wing were rounded off slightly and the ribs simplified. In 2004, for the launch of the DB9, London-based communications agency Imagination, in collaboration with Aston chairman Dr Ulrich Bez, elected to straighten up the feather lines, thicken the wing outline and make the black 'ASTON MARTIN' box bigger. All these changes made the badge stand out because it was now snugly positioned in a recess pressed into the body, instead of sitting proud of the metalwork. Despite all this meddling, if he hadn't died in a house fire in 1981, Mr Davis would still easily recognize his work more than seventy years after he had first drawn it.

Left: James Bond and Aston Martin have been partners since Sean Connery met the DB5 in *Goldfinger* in 1964; below, left: rocket launchers fitted to a Vanquish for the 2002 epic *Die Another Day*; opposite: the new DB9, whose panels now cradle the Aston Martin badge.

AUDI

The four rings of the Audi badge signify the four marques that combined to form Auto Union in 1932 – Audi was one of them; opposite: the dramatic 2002 Avantissimo concept car; below: an up-close image; bottom: an Audi Allroad, one of the company's recent, top-selling cars.

The early 1930s was a critical time for the German manufacturers Audi, DKW, Horch and Wanderer. They all made different types of cars in the Saxony region – from Horch's patrician eight-cylinder limousines, through the mid-range Audi and Wanderer, down to the small front-wheel drive DKW aimed at the impecunious motorist – but none was strong enough to survive independently. So the four companies, under pressure from the State Bank of Saxony, which owned stakes in each of the quartet, merged in 1932 to form one entity: Auto Union.

While the individual marques continued with some rationalization and sharing of components, they were united under a single 'corporate' banner, which took the form of a chain of four identical interlocking circles. The badge's similarity to the symbol for the Olympic Games can surely have been no coincidence; Adolf Hitler chose the company to develop what he anticipated would be

Germany's unbeatable contender on the international Grand Prix circuit, to a design from his favourite engineer and fellow Austrian, Ferdinand Porsche. The car, called an Auto Union, wore the four-ring badge prominently. Auto Union needed the valuable Deutschmarks the German government poured in; despite its combined strength, it made just 27,000 cars in 1934.

After the Second World War, however, only the economical DKWs were made (sometimes sold as Auto Unions), because it was felt there was no demand for the other marques in Germany. The company was bought first by Mercedes-Benz in 1958 and then by Volkswagen in 1965, whereupon the Audi name was dusted off to replace DKW.

So where the DKWs had carried the Auto Union symbol, Audis now did the honours. However, the pre-war 'Audi' script was revived at the same time, with its distinctive elongated right-hand stroke on the capital 'A' and a correspondingly

DKW 750

Opposite: iterations of the pre-1932 and revived 1985–97 Audi badges; opposite, far left: the DKW F2 of 1958 carried the Auto Union emblem; opposite, far left, below: 1930s advertising extolling Auto Union's market-dominating ambitions; opposite, below: the 1980s Audi Quattro used the logo in decal form to indicate its four-wheel drive system.

Below: the Audi Quattro Spyder, an Audi concept car revealed in 1991, was part of the design evolution that saw Audi launch the sensational TT sports car in 1997; right: a whimsical use of the Audi emblem as an exhaust tailpipe on this Quattro design.

angled ascender on the lower case 'd'. Indeed, in 1985 (when Audi changed its corporate name from the baggage-laden Audi NSU Auto Union AG to the more simple Audi AG) this appeared in a brown lozenge on the front wings of Audi's saloons. It was a close approximation of what (in blue) had adorned pre-1939 Audis but, of course, led to the odd situation of the cars carrying two completely different badges. The old-style Audi badge was quietly dropped in 1997.

The four-ring badge has been a chrome fixture on the front and back of every Audi since 1965. But it received new impetus in 1980 with the advent of the Audi Quattro, the four-wheel drive system of which it so perfectly symbolized. Throughout the Audi Quattro's eleven-year life between 1980 and 1991, the aggressive coupé carried a large four-ring logo as a decal on its lower door panels – highly graphic but unthinkable, these days, on a premium-price car.

AUSTIN

Herbert Austin had already established a car division for the Wolseley Sheep Shearing Machine Company when he decided to establish his own firm in Longbridge, Birmingham, England (until recently the home of MG Rover, where locals still call it 'The Austin') in 1905.

The broadly triangular emblem that Austin created as his badge was supposed to represent "rapid, controlled, wheeled motion". The feathery, outstretched wings and the weird, stylized dust at the bottom tip of the triangle signified speed. A road wheel (depicted edge-on) on an axle just above was the motion bit, while a steering column topped with a four-spoke steering wheel signified control. It was too contrived, however, and made little impact, especially as the earliest badge was part of the brass radiator pressing. By the mid-1920s a more exuberant rendition was in use as a separate badge, and a sleeker, elongated version was concocted in 1931.

In March 1947 Austin took the then unusual step of launching a new bonnet mascot. This was a blatant, if inelegant, rip-off of the winged 'B' fitted to Bentleys, for Austin deliberately pitched its A125 Sheerline model as, in the words of boss Leonard Lord, "a poor man's Bentley". The mascot also appeared on all other new Austins until 1958 – even down to the tiny A30 economy car. The 1948 A90 Atlantic was unique in carrying two of these 'flying A's, which were also nicknamed 'kidney-slicers' in gory reference to the damage they could inflict on an unfortunate pedestrian or cyclist. The very last Austin to sport one was an Austin A35 van in 1968.

Not content with a radiator badge and a mascot, Austin had also added a tiny, enamelled badge showing Herbert Austin's own coat of arms to the A90 Atlantic. Knighted in 1936, Lord Austin died in 1941, so perhaps the badge honoured him, but more important was its 'Olde English' appeal to customers in Austin's key Atlantic market – the USA.

In 1950 the badge became a coloured Perspex shield in the centre of the radiator

grille frame on the A70 Hereford, and this gradually supplanted Herbert's Edwardian original until it adorned every Austin by 1960. It could still be found embossed on the plastic steering wheel of the first Austin Allegros in 1973, but shortly afterwards was totally usurped by the 'AUSTIN' script accompanied by the British Leyland or Austin Rover corporate symbols. The Austin name was finally phased out in 1988 after eighty-three years, though it still inspires affection.

BENTLEY

A 'black label' for the 4.5-litre Bentley (below) has endured through to the Continental GT of today, the gearchange of which is shown here (right); bottom: the red enamel badge; opposite: Bentley's mascot, is as aristocratic as its badge.

When Walter Owen Bentley introduced his first model, the 3-litre of 1919, he gave it a very straightforward radiator badge: flowing wings flanking a silver letter 'B' set against the dark-blue background of an enamelled ellipse. To differentiate the 3-litre Speed model, 'W.O.' ordered red enamel for its badge, and green for the Supersports. Buyers adored the cars for their performance and stamina, and 1920s aficionados referred to these three original versions as 'Blue Label', 'Green Label' or 'Red Label'.

Four-and-a-half-litre Bentleys, however, sported a black badge carrying a white 'B'; 4-, 6.5- and 8-litre cars received blue badges, and the Speed Six a green one. W.O. Bentley willingly let customers have bespoke badges; yellow, white and mauve badges are all supposed to have been supplied.

After Rolls-Royce acquired the bankrupt Bentley Motors in 1931, all badges became black-on-chrome. However, the red badge reappeared on the Mulsanne

Turbo in 1982, the green one on 1991 model Bentleys (to celebrate sixty years of Rolls-Royce ownership) and the blue one on the 1995 Bentley Azure. In all this time, the outline and details of the badge have remained remarkably faithful to the 1919 original, despite a graphic tidy-up in about 1933.

Not so Bentley's bewinged radiator cap mascot. Before the Rolls buyout, the three-dimensional 'B' had wings that jutted out on either side, but from 1931, and allegedly with input from renowned motoring artist Frederick Gordon Crosby, the wings flowed out behind the backward-leaning 'B'. The last mascot, which had adopted a forward-leaning aspect several years earlier, was seen on the Bentley T2 in 1980, after which safety legislation meant it was no longer fitted as standard to cars sold in major Western markets.

Bentley's range in 2005 includes the Arnage R and RL with red badges, and the Arnage T and Continental GT with black.

BERTONE

That distinctively kinked 'b' has been a constant on Bertone-designed cars since the 1930s; it has been seen as a simple decal, as on the Lancia Stratos (below), or as a grille emblem on the Bertone Freeclimber SUV (opposite).

Bertone is one of the oldest names in Italian car design and craftsmanship; it has graced everything from Lamborghinis to Fiats. Carrozzeria Bertone ('Carrozzeria' means Coachworks) was founded in 1912 in Turin by Giovanni Bertone as one of a myriad of local bodywork shops serving Fiat and Lancia. His high quality and neat designs set his business apart, however, and his well-educated and urbane son Nuccio joined his father and added style to everything the company did.

Nuccio may have been responsible for the 'b' logo, which was certainly in use as a part of the company's trademark in 1934 when, with a payroll of 150, Carrozzeria Bertone moved to a large new factory. It was the centrepiece of an elaborate, architectural-looking winged device, its bowl kinked downwards to give the impression it was sitting at the prow of a three-dimensional object. A metal version was often fitted to Bertone's stylish bodies just in front of the doors; by 1950 it had lost the extraneous decorations and was now

featured on an upright shield, with a honeycomb enamel background and topped with a gold crown motif.

This badge was fitted to cars with Bertone bodies, both bespoke one-offs and, from 1954, volume models such as the Alfa Romeo Giulietta Sprint and later the Fiat 850 Spider, Simca 1200 coupé and Iso Rivolta. In 1966 one of the most beautiful cars ever was born, the Lamborghini Miura, its body designed by Bertone's talented protégé Marcello Gandini; on this car, the 'b' became a stand-alone chrome cut-out letter, affixed just in front of the rear wheel arch. Subsequent Bertone supercars included the Lancia Stratos, Lamborghini Countach and Ferrari 308GT4. Bertone has also produced a string of stunning concept cars that light up the motor show circuit.

With the consolidation of the European motor industry in the 1980s, Nuccio Bertone turned his plant over to subcontract work for mainstream manufacturers. This led to a proliferation of Bertone's 'b' emblems on European roads, as it lent kudos to Bertone-

built Fiat Ritmo/Strada, Opel Astra and Fiat Punto convertibles.

It was Nuccio Bertone who drove Bertone's prosperity in the post-war period, but he died in 1997. At the time of writing, Bertone's plant faces an uncertain future as Opel/Vauxhall Astra coupé and convertible assembly ends, but its show cars are as spectacular as ever, including the Aston Martin-based Jet sports estate exhibited at the Geneva motor show in 2004.

BMW

Aeroplane engines were the initial business of the Bayerische Motoren Werke (Bavarian Engine Works) in 1916. Pilots of early aircraft said that they could see alternating blue (for sky) and white segments through the propellers spinning frenziedly in front of them; by coincidence, this looked similar to the company's emblem, introduced in 1917. This featured a circle divided into alternating blue and white quarters with the 'BMW' initials above them. But the blue-and-white chequered pattern was actually derived from the Bavarian flag. It was, however, to be another thirteen years before this symbol found its way on to a car.

After the First World War, BMW had been banned from making aircraft engines, and so turned instead to motorcycle engines. In 1923 it built its first complete bike, and in 1928 expanded again by acquiring Dixi Werke of Eisenach. In the face of the Wall Street crash in 1929, BMW ditched Dixi's large cars to concentrate on the DA1, a British Austin Seven produced under

licence, although it also introduced a sporty version of the DA1 and named it the BMW Wartburg after a local castle. The Wartburg sported BMW's aeronautical roundel in its first automotive version. A black ring, piped in yellow on both inner and outer edges, encircled the blue-and-white 'spinning propeller' image. Above it, on the black area, the 'BMW' acronym fanned out in yellow, heavy serif capitals.

As the global economic outlook improved during the 1930s, so did BMW's cars. The Austin-based models soon gave way to a series of high-performance six-cylinder cars such as the 327 and 328, and in 1937 the badge saw its garish yellow replaced by a more serene white.

BMW endured a turbulent time during the 1950s. It was finally rescued by German industrialist Herbert Quandt, who introduced a new product in 1962 in the shape of the BMW 1500 saloon. This was the birth of BMW as we know it today, provider of high-quality saloons with the accent on driver enjoyment. To usher in the new era

came a revised badge, the capital letters now shorn of their dated serifs; this remained unchanged until 1999, when a subtle redesign gave the badge a more three-dimensional appearance.

When BMW officially entered motor sport in 1973, it used its badge as the centrepiece of a new circular logo, with broken sections of mid-blue, purple and bright red in three surrounding bands. It rapidly became a familiar sight on the race track, particularly when the 2002

Below: evidence of the aircraft propeller influence in the BMW logo is amply shown here, although the blue-and-white colours are actually derived from those found on the Bavarian coat of arms – BMW has never seen anything wrong with blurring these two facts.

Far left: the 501 was an expensive BMW saloon of the early 1950s, often referred to by admirers as 'the baroque angel'; left: the popular 2002 of the late 1960s had tail lights that echoed the form of the badge; below: the smooth frontal contours of the BMW 328.

and then the 3.0CSL and 635CSi put in some dazzling performances in touring car races.

At a tangent to the BMW story is EMW – the Eisenach Motoren Werke. This factory had been BMW's main plant in the 1930s, but following the separation of East and West Germany in 1945, it was imprisoned behind the Iron Curtain. To the fury of BMW in Munich, the Eisenach factory started making cars again and badged them as BMWs, and it took seven years to pressure the East Germans to stop it. In 1952, therefore, the old pre-war-style BMWs were renamed EMWs and, although the BMW badge had its 'B' replaced with an 'E', it was essentially the same design, but for one more small detail – the colour scheme was changed, pointedly, from blue to red.

BORGWARD

All Borgwards have worn their badges with unusual prominence, reflecting the red and white city colours of Bremen in a diamond shape. Opposite: a rare Borgward Hansa 2400 from around 1954.

Borgward's most successful model ever was the Isabella sports saloon, shown right in police guise; below: two more variations on the diamond theme, showing how the emblem was artfully integrated into the cars' styling.

Carl Borgward was one of the last mavericks who wagered he could take on the world's established car makers and beat them. He spent the 1920s buying up bankrupt small-scale car and truck factories in Bremen, Germany, including Hansa and Goliath, but there was no actual car bearing the cigar-toting Herr Borgward's name until he modestly renamed one of the many Hansa models he produced, the 2000, after himself in 1939.

Despite the man's indomitable ego, bold plans and inexhaustible energy, Borgward loathed the elaborate badges on his rivals' cars. So he chose a simple diamond badge with the 'BORGWARD' name in capitals across the middle and four triangles – red and white ones diagonally opposite each other, the reds in the top-left and bottom-right quarters – recalling the insignia of the Hansa company that he had absorbed in the 1930s. The red, white and silver colour scheme also happened to

match the coat of arms of the city of Bremen.

Post-war Borgwards, especially the popular Isabella saloon introduced in 1954, wore their badge prominently. An outsize rendition of it dominated the centre of the car's nose, and a toned-down version graced the 1960 Borgward Six, the firm's swansong.

For, despite the fact that some of his cars sold well in post-war Europe, Carl Borgward's company was gradually squeezed out of the market by bigger German players, and went bust in 1961. He died a broken man shortly afterwards, but no one could say he hadn't tried.

BRISTOL

The idiosyncratic British marque Bristol salutes the coat of arms of its namesake city in its sixty-year-old badge, seen below on bonnet and wheel; very few Bristols are sold each year, explaining why the 1984 Brigand saloon and Beaufighter convertible (opposite) have always been rare sights.

The enigmatic British company Bristol Cars celebrates its diamond jubilee in 2005. It was sixty years ago that the Bristol Aeroplane Company formed a car division, after having obtained the manufacturing rights to a BMW 2-litre sports saloon in a carve-up of German car industry assets after the Second World War. It named the car the Bristol 400. Ever since then, Bristol has offered a succession of handbuilt four-seater touring cars, along with a couple of two-seater sports cars, represented today by the Blenheim 3 saloon and the Fighter two-seater.

In 1960 the car-making side was sold to Sir George White and Bristol's London distributor, Tony Crook, and Mr Crook is still the majority owner today. The company long ago gave up advertising its cars, relying instead on a small number of dogged customers who will never drive anything else. It steadfastly refuses to reveal how many cars it makes (although it is dozens a year, rather than hundreds), and claims to have rebuffed several takeover offers. The cars continue to be built at Filton, Bristol, close to the BAe site where they once rubbed shoulders with jet airliners.

Bristol's badge has always been one of the most straightforward, some might say unimaginative. It was on the first Bristol and it's on the latest ones. It features Bristol city's arms, a shield showing a silver castle on a yellow cliff top; on the horizon, a yellow-sailed ship cruises into port on a black sea against a red sky. The 'BRISTOL' name curves around the top in an outer black circle.

The main change in the badge design occurred in 1961, when Bristol stopped making its own engines and began to fit Chrysler V8 engines to its cars, beginning with the 407. At that point the slogan '2-LITRE' was deleted from the lower half of the black circle. Since the mid-1970s launch of the 412, the shield has been seen at the top of an upright black rectangle, with 'BRISTOL' spelt out below it. On the 1994 Blenheim 1, however, it was an oddly misshapen pentagon.

BUGATTI

Ettore Bugatti was born in Milan in 1881, but made his name in Molsheim, Alsace, in 1909, where he established his own car-making business. (Alsace was part of Germany at the time, but became French in 1918.) There he built some 7,850 Bugattis in forty or so models, the most famous being the gigantic Type 41 'Royale' luxury car and the advanced Type 35 racer.

Ettore Bugatti was a highly enigmatic character. He lived in what motoring historian David Burgess-Wise has called "feudal splendour": his factory and home were on the same estate, and he would often ride around the works on horseback. Bugatti certainly knew how to make an impact. A trademark of his often beautiful cars was a distinctive radiator, somewhere between a horseshoe and an egg in outline shape.

For his badge, Bugatti personally selected a geometrically perfect ellipse, with an aspect ratio of two-to-one. On a red background was the word 'BUGATTI' in block capitals, enamelled white with a black drop-shadow, and above it in black was his 'EB' monogram, a formalized rendition of the way he hurriedly initialled documents. Around the edge in a narrow, white-enamelled band was a continuous chain of tiny squares. The badge remained unchanged right through to 1951, four years after Bugatti's death, when production of the Molsheim series petered out. The only change, at some stage early on, was to turn those perimeter squares into dots.

A Bugatti car was revived with the shortlived EB110 in 1991, but such is the enduring power of the name that Volkswagen snapped up the brand in 1998. Its Veyron concept supercar was unveiled in 2000, but is not yet on sale. Volkswagen has remained very faithful to Bugatti's original, anxious not to upset well-informed Bugatti connoisseurs who have doggedly guarded the marque's heritage for decades.

BUICK

Buick's 'tri-shield' emblem, basically three shields inside a circle, can be traced directly to the ancestral coat of arms of the car maker's Scottish founder, David Buick. General Motors, partly founded on Buick's success, would do well not to alter it: a study of the impact of corporate symbols in the early 1990s by US identity group Schechter found that the tri-shield elicited a 53% 'positive image' in the minds of consumers, an astonishingly good result compared to most logos. Nevertheless, today's badge is the latest of many incarnations.

Buick first used the Buick family crest as a bonnet badge on its 1937 models. In the mid-1930s, General Motors styling researcher Ralph Pew had found an abbreviated description of the arms of the Buick family – then spelled Buik – in an 1851 edition of *Burke's Heraldry* in the Detroit Public Library. It read: "Gu. A bend chequy, ar. and az. betw. a Buck's head erazed in chief, and a cross coupéd and pierced, or, in base". There was no illustration, but the description was carefully interpreted by

Pew into a badge: a red shield with a chequered silver and azure diagonal line running top left to bottom right, an antlered deer's head with a jagged neckline in the upper right corner of the shield and a gold cross in the lower left one. The cross had a hole in the centre with the red of the shield showing through.

The shield was modernized in 1939 by making it longer and narrower, and again in 1942 when classic heraldic symbols garnished the top and bottom. In 1949 the crest was widened once more to match the broader, lower bonnet and grille styling.

The badge underwent its most radical change on 1960-season Buicks. In place of one shield, a tri-shield design appeared, representing the three models then offered – LeSabre, Invicta and Electra. All the original crest symbols and decorative colours were retained, except that the shield was seen overlapping and in triplicate in red, white (later silver-grey) and blue.

In 1975 Buick decided to do something

The changing face of Buick, from top to bottom, between the 1930s and the 1950s, typically saw the badge subsumed into the frontal design; the car in the centre is the 1938 Buick Y-Job, one of the world's first concept cars.

different. The Skyhawk coupé featured the circular emblem of a hawk in airborne attack on its prey and 'BUICK' as a separate, block-letter nameplate. It was well received, and in 1976 spread to other models. Later, the emblem homed in on the hawk's head.

By the late 1980s Buick had reverted back to the historic tri-shield, the hawk was dropped, and the red, silver and blue shields made a comeback; no deer's head, cross or chequered pattern on the diagonal, but otherwise just about recognizable.

For identity on 1906 cars, a large brass 'Buick' script was affixed to the mesh radiator grille (it's been seen on 1905 cars but is thought by experts to have been fitted retrospectively). The same script framed inside (and overlapping the edges of) a blue rectangle with a thick white border dates from 1913, and appeared on the faceplate of the Boyce Motometer temperature gauge, which was fitted as standard to radiator caps of Buicks prior

to 1927. By the 1930s it was a regular feature on radiator shells too.

In case you were wondering, how did a Scot come to found one of American motoring's most venerable car brands? Buick was born in Arbroath, Scotland, on 17 September 1854. His family moved to the USA when he was two and he grew up in Detroit, becoming an entrepreneur in the plumbing trade (he is said to have invented the enamelled bath). By 1900 he had built his own car design, and formed the Buick Auto-Vim and Power Co. to exploit it. That evolved into the Buick Motor Co. of Detroit in 1903, when the firm was purchased by Flint Wagon Works in Flint, Michigan. The company (which still included David Buick) completed thirty-seven Buick cars in 1904, but by 1908 – when new proprietor William Durant used Buick as the cornerstone of General Motors – it was making 8,000 units annually and claimed to be the US auto industry leader. Also in 1908, David Buick left to pursue other ventures, but died a poor man in 1929.

Left, top to bottom: Buick was among the most enthusiastic exponents of chrome decoration, which generally won the visual battle for attention from the car's emblem; key Buick distinguishing features were the gleaming 'portholes' on the front wings.

Below: the svelte lines of the 1963 Buick Riviera were a world removed from the marque founder's origins in the plumbing business – this is American car styling at its most accomplished.

CADILLAC

If you can take your eyes away from the magnificent mascot adorning the Cadillac V16 to the right, you'll notice the Cadillac emblem in one of its more modest guises: the Cadillac logo is shown below as part of an unusually value-focused press advertisement.

Many car badges and logos have heraldic roots, but few have been turned into automotive icons as convincingly as Cadillac's. Nor, for that matter, have many been as consistently applied as this heavyweight of American motoring. The only blip in its otherwise splendid progress from 1905 to now was, ironically, on the most iconic of all Cadillacs, the 1959 models with their towering, spaceship fins. Here, the Cadillac badge became a cartoonish caricature of itself – a mere nod to heritage at a time of unparalleled American confidence.

Until 1905 Cadillac's metal signature on its single-cylinder cars was a brass cut-out of the 'Cadillac' word fixed to the radiator grille – drawn with panache (as evinced by the flash begun by the tail of the final 'c' and pulled back extravagantly to underline the word) yet not vastly different from that of many contemporary rivals. But in that year, the company boldly grabbed the symbol of the very founding father of Detroit – America's burgeoning 'Motown' –

from under the noses of its competitors, and made it its very own.

The Cadillac 'crest' is the coat of arms of Antoine de la Mothe Cadillac, a member of the Toulouse-based family who founded the city of Detroit in 1701. The fledgling company adopted his name in 1902; by August 1906 it had registered his family crest as its own too. It has two elements: a shield with a coronet sitting on top of it. This crown, with a pearl on each of its seven pinnacles, symbolizes Cadillac and his relationship with the six ancient courts of France.

The shield is divided into four quarters. In the top-left and bottom-right areas are the arms of the de la Mothe family – a black horizontal bar with two birds above it and one below, set on a gold background. The legless, beakless birds are 'merlettes', modelled on martins and, according to the medieval historian Guillaume, "given ... to younger brothers to put them in mind that in order to raise themselves they are to look to the wings of

virtue and merit, and not to the legs, having but little land to set their feet on". Seen as a trio, they represent the Holy Trinity, and were usually bestowed by the ancient School of Heralds to truly fearless crusaders. The colour scheme, black against gold, denotes wisdom and riches. The lateral bar was another award for valiant crusade conduct; it implies the holder is always ready to defend public welfare.

The opposite quarters, subdivided again into four, with red panels alternating with blue/silver striped ones featuring more lateral dividing bars, were probably added after a favourable marriage that increased the family's estates. Red stands for "prowess and boldness in action", silver for "purity, charity, virtue and plenty", and blue for knightly valour.

Here was a heavy burden of history, but it suited the increasingly extravagant coachwork sported by Cadillacs in the 1920s and 1930s. As a circular badge, it was set off by a horseshoe-shaped laurel

garland encircling the lower half, although this was discarded in 1925 when the badge changed from being mounted in a circle to a shield-shaped plinth. Three years later chrome wings were added and, towards the end of the 1930s, the badge was incorporated into a large, decorative chrome medallion from which the crest itself was detachable. Post-war models sported it cradled in the valley of a large chrome 'V', to advertise the V8 power beneath.

On 1958, 1959 and 1960 Cadillacs, the crest (and the 'V') was flattened into a thin, chrome pastiche of the original to suit the long, low look of the cars themselves. Cadillac had introduced its first tail fin in 1949, and they reached their massive peak in 1959. By 1965, however, they had been eradicated from the cars, and the badge was back in its rightful, square-rigged position.

In 1975 models the crest made a sudden leap from the prow of the bonnet to become a free-standing bonnet emblem, variously provided as a coloured emblem or a stylized metal 'skeleton', but in both cases framed by a resurrected chrome wreath.

In 1999 show cars such as the Evoq began to represent the crown and its pinnacles as little more than a wavy, chrome-edged line on top of the shield. The Cien show car of 2002, built to celebrate Cadillac's one hundreth birthday, discarded it altogether, the shield having just a pitched chrome bar at the top; this style was first seen in showrooms on the 2002 CTS saloon. Despite the dozens of variations on the Cadillac crest over the preceding century, this is the most radical – almost shocking – change since 1916–18, when those merlettes were for some inexplicable reason briefly replaced by white swans and there were nine, rather than seven, pearls!

CATERHAM

The Caterham story is a tale of design purity and longevity. The company has made exciting sports cars since 1973, when it acquired the manufacturing rights to the Lotus Seven two-seater. It had been intimately familiar with the cars since 1959, when it sold its first one; since 1967 it had been the sole Seven concessionaire in the UK. Every Caterham since 1973 has been a development of that classic design.

How did this ideal weekend fun car come to be named after an unremarkable commuter town in Surrey, England? Caterham Car Sales noticed that its customers referred to its new progeny as the 'Caterham Seven' instead of the Lotus Seven, and the name simply stuck. Company founder Graham Nearn now freely admits it wasn't something he would have chosen, so it was a decisive vote for the power of the customer!

Part of Caterham's deal with Lotus was that it had to change the Seven's badge. This it did by inverting Lotus's famous camshaft lobe shape so that the sharper end was at the bottom. Then it stacked the word 'SUPER' above the figure '7' on a bright yellow background, and set it all in a black circle.

That was at the beginning. In 1990 Caterham added a yellow outer band edged in green with 'CATERHAM' arrayed around the upper half. This was purely to better communicate the brand to curious onlookers, although some would say that, as one of the most enduring car shapes on the roads today, it hardly needed it. The yellow lobe remained, but the background infill also changed to green.

In 1992 a special edition called the JPE came with a new badge, in black on a gold background, and this gave rise to a new, general Caterham version: a simple black '7' in the silver lobe outline set in a black circle, while the 'SUPER' and 'CATERHAM' were jettisoned. A further spin-off was the black-on-chrome badge on the Caterham Seven Sprint, with 'SUPER' and '7' in the lobe and 'SPRINT' nestling underneath it.

In 2004 Caterham unveiled an artfully revised range, with new Cosworth engines; the badge featured a yellow outer band, green inner circle, and a gold '7' shape just like the lobe of old. Around the top it read 'CATERHAM', around the bottom '16 VALVE'.

CHEVROLET

smooth as quicksilver...
and quick as they come...the '57 Chevrolet!

General Motors is seeking to make the Chevrolet badge familiar worldwide by imbuing a range of Korean-built models, possibly to include the S3K opposite, with the heritage of cars such as the iconic 1957 Chevy, shown in the advertisement (left).

It wasn't Swiss-born racing driver Louis Chevrolet who came up with what's called the Chevrolet 'bow tie' badge (odd, that, because it looks only like a very badly tied one): it was his backer and business partner, William Durant, who used Chevrolet and Buick as the foundations for General Motors in 1908.

That year, apparently, when Durant was on a business trip to Paris, he took a liking to the wallpaper pattern in his hotel room. He tore off a tiny section and put it in his wallet, thinking it might make a good badge.

However, a conflicting account came from Durant's wife when she was interviewed by author Lawrence Gustin in 1973. She recalled a holiday in Hot Springs, Virginia, around 1912. Her husband, she said, was inspired by a newspaper illustration. "We were in a suite reading the papers, and he saw this design and said: 'I think this would be a very good emblem for the Chevrolet.'" It may have been an advertisement for a brand of firelighters called Coalettes, which had a very similar trademark shape.

However, there is no doubt that the badge was Durant's idea. Margery Durant recorded in her 1929 book *My Father* that he "drew nameplates on pieces of paper at the dinner table. I think it was between the soup and the fried chicken one night that he sketched out the design used on the Chevrolet car to this day."

The badge made its debut on a Chevrolet car in 1913. The square central section and the bar with its diagonally opposing slant was framed in white, while 'CHEVROLET', also in white, sat on a dark-blue background. In the space above and below the words, a short, white horizontal keyline helped frame the '-VRO-' letters.

Having created such a distinctive logo, it became increasingly lost among the elaborate chromework embellishing Chevrolets from the 1930s to 1960s. By the 1970s, and in common with other US brands, the fusty old badge had mostly been replaced by individual liveries for Chevrolet sub-brands such as Corvette and Camaro. With the Citation and Celebrity of the early 1980s, however, the outline at least returned in a bullish manner, sometimes in red plastic to denote a sporty variant.

After a century during which Chevrolet has been as American as apple pie, General Motors is belatedly turning it into a truly global brand, extending it into Europe for the first time, for example, as the new nameplate on South Korean Daewoo cars. Interestingly, the new Chevrolet-labelled cars from Korea will also feature just the 'bow tie' outline as a gold-coloured plaque; even customers in markets totally new to the brand are deemed able to recognize them from that.

CHRYSLER

Opposite: the modern face of Chrysler is shown here in the Crossfire model, sporting the 'rosette' badge revived in 1998; bottom: the heavily 'retro' design, shown below on the grille of the Voyager, evokes Chrysler's 1930s heydays of the Art Deco Airflow model.

The rise of Walter Percy Chrysler from floor-sweeper on the Union Pacific Railroad to car-making magnate was meteoric. As superintendent of the entire Chicago Great Western Railroad in 1906 at the age of just thirty, Chrysler managed to get together enough money to buy his first car, a Locomobile. He then spent the next three months of his spare time dismantling it in his barn to find out how everything worked. This was before he had even learned to drive.

Chrysler finally entered the car industry on his own account in 1923, employing the consultant engineering partnership of Zeder Skelton Breer to fine-tune the large four-cylinder car for America's customers. This gave Walter Chrysler more time to consider those customers, and he came to the conclusion that many would be from the farming community. He is, consequently, thought to have decided on a red-and-gold 'ribbon seal' badge for Chrysler cars because he felt its similarity to a rosette pinned to a championship-winning bull at a country fair would strike the right note. It would, most likely, say the right things to city dwellers from rural backgrounds too.

Chrysler apparently added that the circles within the seal outline represented his car's wheels, and the lightning flashes above and below the diagonally slanted 'CHRYSLER' lettering symbolized speed. However, as engineer Fred Zeder, possibly the actual designer of the badge, nursed ambitions to be a car maker himself, the twin thunderbolts are perhaps really meant to evoke the letter 'Z'! The Chrysler design team also devised a radiator cap mascot based on the mythical wings of Mercury, and by the early 1930s the seal was combined with stylized wings in an ornate badge ensemble.

In 1955, and with Walter Percy dead for fifteen years, Chrysler's head of styling, Virgil Exner, had had enough of the folksy ribbon seal. His car design influences were from jet fighters and spacecraft, not prize livestock. He eliminated the badge

Below: the 1963 Chrysler
Turbine, the world's only
production jet-engined
road car came along at
the time the company
was jettisoning its folksy
old rosette for its groovy
new 'Pentastar'
(opposite).

completely, preferring to custom-design the badging on each car around his futuristic 'Forward Look' theme of two bisecting chevrons, and a flowing 'Chrysler' script logo in chrome.

However, with the flamboyant Exner's retirement in 1962, Chrysler Corporation chairman Lynn Townsend had a rethink and decided the cars and the company needed a corporate coming-together of identity. He hired New York design consultants Lippincott & Margulies to manage the task and, after examining seven hundred ideas, he chose the cringingly entitled 'Pentastar', a white five-pointed star set against a cool blue pentagon. It quickly made its way on to the bonnet of every Chrysler and, as the company expanded in Europe, it displaced Hillman, Humber, Sunbeam and Simca badges too. However, there was no hidden nuance to the Pentastar: it was just a neat and highly recognizable, if rather soulless and two-dimensional, geometric shape.

There was a surprise in store in 1998. A matter of months before the shock announcement of the takeover of Chrysler by Germany's Daimler-Benz, the US company announced a return to the ribbon seal on all Chrysler-brand cars, in a version remarkably faithful to Walter Chrysler's original. "The gold seal badge emphasizes that we are a forward-thinking company that maintains a deep respect for our history", said Tim Adams, then president of Chrysler Europe.

The Pentastar lived on a while longer as the company's corporate thumbprint, but eventually that reverted to the ribbon seal at the same time as the cars themselves received an elaborate revival of the winged edition. It looked particularly appropriate on the strongly retro PT Cruiser. Like the wheels in the rosette itself, the Chrysler badge had come full circle.

CITROËN

The 2003 Citroën C-Airdream concept (opposite) is returning to the outsize 'double chevron' logo that was such a feature of the pre-war Traction Avant models (far right and far right, below); Citroën's original logo style (right) was current from 1919 to 1955.

André Citroën's passion for publicity was second only to his devotion to industrial manufacturing. Born in Paris in 1876, he was fascinated by a wooden gear pattern with double helical teeth invented by a business contact in Poland, and eventually set up a factory in St Denis, France, to make them in steel. These smooth-running gears made him a fortune (a version was even used on the steering gear of the Titanic). After the Second World War, Citroën decided he wanted to be a car manufacturer too, and imported American mass-production techniques to transform the shambolic car industry methods then widespread across Europe.

His first car, the Type A of 1919, was tough, well equipped and wildly successful. As it drove towards you, there was no mistaking it. On the prow of its radiator shell was Citroën's badge, an elongated octagonal outline in dark blue framing a yellow oval, with two of those helical gear teeth set right across the centre as twin yellow chevrons, and the 'CITROËN' legend in the lower, enclosed blue portion.

But that wasn't the only place you saw it in 1920s France, because Citroën gave the government 150,000 signs to help improve the country's archaic roadside directions. In a staggering display of self-publicity, they were all oval in shape and bore the Citroën double-chevron logo prominently across them.

The radical Traction Avant range of 1934 dispensed with the badge, however. Instead, two enormous chevrons were incorporated right across the centre of the cars' radiator grilles. Getting this car into production bankrupted Citroën, and the stress killed him in 1935. So he never knew the 2CV, nor the incredible DS of 1955. This shark-like saloon was so distinctive that it didn't even have a bonnet badge; rather, on the boot were bolted two chrome chevrons, now with no frame at all and their ends tapering to pin-sharp points. It was the work of the gifted DS designer himself, Flaminio Bertoni.

The stark and beautifully simple Citroën symbol reinterpreted by sculptor Flaminio Bertoni on the shark-like DS (left and below) he designed.

The iterations differ in their detail applications but, as these three cars demonstrate, the Citroën badge sticks closely to the symbolism of the gear teeth from which company founder André Citroën first made his fortune.

This automotive trademark, one of the most recognizable ever since, is still found on all Citroëns today. One interesting variation was the 1983–92 BX and the earlier AX and XM models, where the badge was offset to the far right of the bonnet edge. In 1985, however, the firm's corporate livery for documents and communications finally changed from André Citroën's preferred blue and yellow to red and white.

Beginning with the C4, launched in 2004, the two chevrons have now been totally merged with the grille to form one enormous new rendition of the Citroën emblem.

DAEWOO

The Daewoo badge and also the cars' nose designs are simplified versions of the company's corporate logo suggesting the six continents and seven seas. The Daewoo Leganza (below) was one of the company's many 1990s offerings.

Daewoo's career as a stand-alone car manufacturer has been brief and turbulent. Founded in South Korea as a textile company by Woo-Choong Kim in 1967, in the 1970s it expanded tangentially by building General Motors cars under licence. The culmination of this arrangement was a deal that saw one of them (known elsewhere as the Opel Kadett) sold in the USA as the Pontiac Le Mans. This was hugely to General Motors' benefit because labour rates in South Korea were low, but it bolstered Daewoo's confidence to think that it had true bargaining power with its American partner. It did not, and the contract ended abruptly in 1994.

Undaunted, Daewoo (pronounced 'Day-oo', and meaning 'great universe') then switched its focus to Europe, exporting a version of the Kadett as the Daewoo Nexia as well as the Espero, a redesigned Opel Ascona. They carried the Daewoo logo out into world markets for the first time, one heavily larded with global ambition.

On paper and signage a slightly flattened aquamarine circle represented the earth. Rooted at the bottom of this, six white strands rose up and fanned out to suggest the six continents, while the five thin empty areas and the two larger areas at each end implied the planet's seven seas. A simplified, chrome version shaped like a moth with outstretched wings adorned the cars.

The products were dynamically mediocre but proved reasonably popular, particularly in the UK after they went on sale in 1995. With European input, Daewoo launched the attractive Matiz city car in 1998; the subsequent new models were given grilles that were, in effect, outsize versions of the badge outline.

Alas, Daewoo's massively inflated corporate ego popped in 2001 when it was declared insolvent. The company's old nemesis, General Motors, acquired most of its asset base, renaming it GM Daewoo in 2002 and launching several new cars. There's also a new badge, a

bolder but more compact take on the first one ("modernized and sharpened up", said a company spokesman), which makes it more like a seashell than a moth, but the matching grille has gone, ushering in a new, more modest era for Daewoo. In 2004 it was announced that the Daewoo name would be supplanted by Chevrolet.

DAF

Daf's badges have always been simple, whether on the later 66 (bottom) or its earliest Daffodil 33 (opposite); Daf cars' unique selling point was always their 'two pedal' automatic transmission, as illustrated below.

Until the debut of the Daf Daffodil, automatic gearboxes had generally remained the preserve of drivers of large, expensive cars. But this little vehicle, with its compact dimensions and thrifty, air-cooled 600 cc engine, was ideal for urban drivers who, perhaps, had been deterred from driving by having to master gearbox and clutch skills. The Daf used a new type of automatic system called a continuously variable transmission. It had one forward and one reverse speed, and only brake and accelerator pedals, and so was extremely easy to drive, even if at a 60 mph maximum it was somewhat tardy.

Launched at the 1958 Amsterdam motor show, the Daf instantly became the first Dutch production car of any consequence since the demise of Spyker in 1925. It was built in Eindhoven by truck and trailer specialist Van Doorne's Automobielfabrieken, from which the marque name is derived.

There was no elaborate badge logo for Daf. Identity consisted of a simple lower-case 'daf' script in delicate chrome outline on the bonnet. A straight(-ish) line linked the bowls of the 'd' and 'a' to the 'f', with its short, zigzagged retreat to give the final letter a double crossbar.

More models followed in the late 1960s, starting with the neatly styled and more powerful Daf 44 in 1967. In 1968 the chrome script was discarded; all Dafs henceforth had a very simple nameplate attached to the grille, generally allied to a model name to read 'DAF 33' (the updated Daffodil), 'DAF 44' or 'DAF 55'. The launch of the Daf 66 in 1972, however, saw the appellations dropped and 'DAF' move to the centre of the grille.

Volvo acquired Daf in 1974; the little cars continued until 1978, but they were now renamed Volvo 66 and given the Volvo grille and badge usually found on much larger vehicles. They remained continuously variable automatics until the very end.

E NEW, FAST

LLY-AUTOMATIC

DAIHATSU

There is no mystery to this capital 'D'; whether as a grille badge (bottom) or a chrome bonnet emblem (opposite, on the Copen sports car), it simply stands for Daihatsu, which equates to 'Osaka Motor'. The elaborate crest on the 1964 Compagno (below) is, in fact, totally meaningless.

There is no reason why you should have heard of the Hatsudoki Seizo Co., a diesel engine company established in Osaka, Japan, in 1907. But in 1948 it changed its name to the Daihatsu Motor Company ('Daihatsu' being a compound of the Japanese for Osaka and motor), and three years later launched a three-wheeled car.

Daihatsu's output was focused primarily on Japan until, in 1964, it unveiled a modest but competent family car called the Berlina 800. Daihatsu had ambition aplenty (renamed the Compagno, the car was the first Japanese vehicle marketed in the UK) but zero recognition. This is probably the reason why Daihatsu concocted an almost laughable pastiche of a badge for the car, a faux-heraldic shield divided into four quarters – top left and bottom right in dark blue, their opposite numbers in red – and bounded by a white frame and then a thick chrome lip. In the top-left space was a capital 'D' executed with a signature-like flourish, while in the bottom right was a diamond split in the middle and with a

horizontal bar either side of it. These symbols were in silver, as was the word 'DAIHATSU' in a black band full-width across the top.

Perhaps sensing that this meaningless emblem was causing nothing but confusion, Daihatsu went the other way with its 1966 Fellow city car, fitting a square badge with a capital 'D' tilted dynamically to the left and with a double stem to give the impression that the character is raised up from the badge surface. As a chrome outline, it was often set against an upright rectangle, circle or, as today, an ellipse, with the radiator grille or boot lid paintwork showing through. In all Daihatsu paper communications and corporate livery, however, the 'D' symbol is in white against a bright red square.

An interesting aside is that Saab used the Daihatsu name on 1967 prototypes of its 99 saloon, to trick onlookers during public road tests. No Daihatsu had ever been registered in Sweden, and engineers made a crude 'daihatsu' script by adapting badges from other Saab models.

DAIMLER

The cornerstone of the British car industry, Daimler was founded in 1896. Its products were widely demonstrated in road trials, and many customers were inspired to buy a Daimler after the Prince of Wales (later King Edward VII) acquired his in 1901. Although Gottlieb Daimler did lend his name to the venture, within months the British cars were totally different to those made by his German firm that became Daimler-Benz.

Daimler's preoccupation with the nascent automotive technology appears to have left little time to devise a badge. From 1904, however, British Daimlers were distinguishable because of the metal cooling fins on top of the radiator mounted at the front of the car. A cowling to cover these dangerously hot items was fluted to mirror the hidden components, and a wavy pattern to the radiator grille remained a Daimler hallmark for virtually a century.

Even by 1909 Daimler still didn't have a badge, but a trademark was devised that year that was highly distinctive. 'Daimler' was spelt out elegantly but conservatively, apart from the right-hand curve of the capital 'D', the top stroke of which continues up and round, doubling back on itself to soar across the whole word before curving gently back round to tuck its tail neatly under it, coming to a pointed end just under the 'm'.

With the fluted radiator grille a positive talking point among Edwardian drivers, Daimler was reluctant to use its logo on its cars, fitting a large cast version only to the front of trucks and buses. Not until 1960 and the launch of the SP250 sports car did a Daimler car carry the badge on its nose, and that was the last. In this version, the tail emanating from the 'D' terminated under the 'e', so that the word 'ENGLAND' could be inserted below 'Daimler'.

Thereafter, Jaguar owned Daimler. The 1962 Daimler V8 250 saloon, effectively a Jaguar Mk2 with a Daimler V8 engine, was given a rather half-hearted bonnet mascot in the form of a streamlined letter 'D', while

the car that supplanted it, the 1967 Sovereign saloon, was the first Daimler with a circular bonnet badge. This was merely the characterful, curly 'D' taken from the original Daimler script, set in silver on a black background; it has been seen on every Daimler since, including the majestic DS420 limousine so beloved of the late Queen Mother.

DELAGE

Les 3 litres

"NORMALE" 1 CARBURATEUR
"OLYMPIC" 3 CARBURATEURS

SÉDUISANTES

FOUGUEUSES

Opposite: the DI was a great success for Delage in the 1920s, while the GL (below) was an attempt to take on Rolls-Royce, its badge more aristocratic to match. This brochure cover (left) promotes the later 3-litre models built under Delahaye auspices.

A much-admired sporting marque of the vintage period, the simplicity of the Delage badge gave it plenty of impact. This was exactly what company founder Louis Delage aimed for, and he was stout in his resolve not to alter it in the face of frequent suggestions from buyers and colleagues for something more glamorous.

The badge, designed by Delage's chief engineer, Augustin Legros, in 1905 was a gilded metal oval with a thin silver or brass frame and the 'Delage' name filling the space inside, on a dark-blue background; the letters increased and then decreased in size from left to right. The only concession to exuberance was the lettering's punchy bulge in the centre, boosted by the fact that it was gently domed. Some cars built just before the First World War had badges with a white background.

Delage set out to build high-quality cars from day one, and a racing programme begun in 1906 soon brought results, culminating in 1927 in the Grand Prix world championship for its straight-eight racers.

The company had a major success in the 2-litre DE and DI models in the 1920s, and tried to take on Rolls-Royce with the 6-litre GL and GLS, but in 1935 it was almost bankrupt, and the brand name was bought by rival French marque Delahaye. The last Delage-badged car was sold in 1953, ending a line that had, during the 1930s, become synonymous with high performance and beautiful coachwork.

Despite Louis Delage's resistance to tampering with his badge, there are variations. The DISS sports models made between 1925 and 1926 had the same basic badge but with a pale-blue background and dark-blue lettering. The mighty GL incorporated the standard Delage logo in the centre of a tall rectangle, coloured either white or black, with the elongated 'DL' initials of the proud Louis Delage behind it in red. And the post-1945 cars had a narrower radiator grille with a smaller Delage badge that was, by now, chrome-plated instead of gilded.

DELOREAN

There is a strong sense of 1980s corporate excess in the chunky DeLorean badge. The three fat initials, seemingly chiselled from solid steel to match the finish of the DeLorean DMC-12's low-slung bodywork, wouldn't look out of place in an old Michael Douglas movie, where they might be affixed to the façade of a fictitious bank, media firm or computer corporation that turns out to be rife with skulduggery.

The saga of John Z. De Lorean's ill-fated sports car, coincidently, happens to live up to this scenario. Controversy surrounded De Lorean and his car from the project's inception in 1978 to well past its 1982 demise, and even now the whereabouts of some £80 million backing from the British government for the firm's Northern Ireland plant continue to be debated.

DeLorean built 8,550 DMC-12 cars in its short life. It was a coupé with Italian styling by Giorgetto Giugiaro, a mid-mounted V6 Renault engine, stainless steel bodywork, gullwing doors and a $19,500 price tag in the USA, which turned out to be its only market. Its badge, carried in the centre of a narrow, horizontal radiator grille, spelt out 'DMC' for DeLorean Motor Company and formed a perfect visual palindrome as the stem of the capital 'D' was omitted.

The cars, first delivered in 1981, initially sold strongly but their poor quality and underwhelming performance, on top of an economic recession, took their toll and the enterprise had been wound up by 1982. The ramifications of the missing millions, however, rumbled on for years; John De Lorean – formerly a star executive at General Motors – was implicated in drugs scandals and in 2000 was declared bankrupt. Surviving DeLorean cars have achieved cult status, especially after they were used in the *Back To The Future* movie series. DeLorean memorabilia is popular, too, the biggest item bearing the cursed logo probably being a two-metre-long, stainless-steel-and-black-carpet sign that once graced the DeLorean HQ foyer in Dunmurry, County Antrim. A local enthusiast saved it for posterity.

DE TOMASO

It sounds Italian, and the De Tomaso factory is indeed based in Modena – the heart of Italy's supercar (and balsamic vinegar) region – but Alejandro de Tomaso hailed from Argentina. This is celebrated in his cars' badge, which employs the Argentinian national flag turned on its end, its two light-blue and one white stripe framed in a rectangle with a heavy black border that curves round the corners. In the centre, a black symbol represents the iron tool used by generations of the Ceballos family (his mother's clan, descended from Spanish viceroys who governed Argentina from 1590) to brand their horses and, later, cattle on their estate at the foot of the Andes. Rather conveniently, it is shaped like a capital T.

His family were still wealthy Argentinian land-owners when De Tomaso, a keen racing driver, decided to emigrate to Italy and set up his own racing car workshop in Modena in 1963. One early car, the Vallelunga, was showcased by New York's Museum of Modern Art, but it was the De Tomaso Mangusta in 1966 that really set people talking. It was a beautiful and powerful mid-engined supercar that challenged the established dominance of Ferrari and Maserati.

De Tomaso's Pantera and Deauville models later bore the branding symbol alone as a fixture to their radiator grilles. His own cars took a back seat in the 1970s, however, as his empire expanded to include Maserati, Innocenti, Moto Guzzi and Benelli. As his eponymous brand had a certain 'supercar' cachet, he signed licensing deals that saw De Tomaso livery appear on special versions of the Daihatsu Charade and Dodge Omni.

De Tomaso died in May 2003, but his family-owned company still makes a small number of Guara sports cars each year, and is involved in a joint venture with Russia's UAZ to produce a version of its 4x4 vehicle for the southern European market.

DFP

There are dozens of also-ran marques from the pre-First World War period whose badges were as dull and generic as their products. DFP, however, was slightly different.

Monsieurs Doriot, Flandrin and Parant were three French partners whose factory at Courbevoie, Paris, turned out a variety of small cars using other manufacturers' engines from 1906 until 1910. But in 1911 they decided to make their own motors, including a 2-litre four-cylinder and a 3-litre six-cylinder. They were very decent, if unremarkable, cars, but they were soon being sold in Britain by two brothers, W.O. and H.M. Bentley.

The Bentleys, however, did more than this, tuning and racing DFP cars to create a glamorous image that was the envy of rivals. Much of their success was based on using novel aluminium pistons. In 1913 one of their much-modified 2-litre DFPs covered half a mile at a timed 89.7 mph (the world land speed record at the time was 141 mph).

In recognition, the lozenge-shaped DFP badge not only included the founders' initials but mentioned 'LONDON' as well as 'PARIS' as their location, and sported the silhouette of a slinky-looking greyhound, streaking along and wearing a collar. It was a bold and comparatively unpretentious badge, and customers could order a similarly athletic greyhound radiator mascot too. The company motto was 'Fidel et vit' – honesty and speed.

The 3-litre was the real dog, slow and unreliable, but the First World War intervened before the Bentleys could get to work on that engine. When it was over, DFP struggled along for a further eight years. Walter Owen Bentley, however, took the basic 3-litre DFP and based his design for the first 3-litre Bentley of 1919 on its potential. A legend was, falteringly, about to be born.

DODGE

The ram symbol has appeared intermittently on Dodges since 1932, shown opposite as Avard Fairbanks's sculpture and below in today's incarnation; the controversial 'double-D' badge is also shown opposite.

Dodge's badge is about to become a whole lot more familiar: for years virtually unknown outside the USA, the marque is being launched across Europe by owner DaimlerChrysler. This means that people are bound to wonder at the bas-relief emblem of a stylized ram's head, curly horns and all, gazing out from a shield-shaped frame.

The ram badge was first worn on a Dodge in 1932, supposedly chosen by Walter P. Chrysler (Chrysler acquired Dodge in 1928) because he liked the idea of the big-horn sheep as a symbolic 'king of the trail'. It also suited a brand whose one-word sales slogan was 'Dependability', and whose founders were famously indomitable. It took the form of a bonnet ornament based on a sculpture by Avard Fairbanks. The animal's appearance on subsequent Dodge vehicles was intermittent, although the model name Ram itself was attached to a range of vans and trucks in the 1960s and 1970s, and was marketed with renewed

vigour when the powerful Dodge Ram pick-up was relaunched in 1994.

The ram portrays a less controversial message than John and Horace Dodge's first emblem. Their cars first appeared in 1914 bearing a circular badge. In a black band around the edge were the words 'DODGE BROTHERS' and 'DETROIT-U-S-A' and in the middle an image of the globe, the sea blue-enamelled on a brass base. In the centre the 'DB' letters were combined into a monogram. Superimposed across the globe were two deltas, the Greek letter for 'D', implying again the two Dodge brothers, but they bisected each other so that they represented the Star of David symbol. While everyone could tell that the global image hinted at the Dodge brothers' ambitions, the star convinced industry observers that the brothers were Jewish, or at least that they had secret Jewish financial backers. None of it was true, and the deltas were anyway coloured white and black to dispel such ideas. Still, in the fevered atmosphere of the

late 1930s, the badge was deemed a liability; it was dropped in 1939.

Then began a long period when Dodges were identified just by numerous 'DODGE' font logos, and even by Chrysler 'Pentastar' badges on many models by the late 1980s. It seems that only the brand's incorporation into the multinational DaimlerChrysler organization in 1999 has released it from being an indistinct Chrysler clone.

DONKERVOORT

The Donkervoort badge celebrates the man who, in 1978, established what is probably the most successful Dutch sports car firm of all time: Joop Donkervoort. As you might expect from a car with sporting ambitions, the emblem is a winged device, with six gold horizontal ribs sticking out on either side and dropping in size the lower they go. But they're not the main event: these are the two large 'JD' initials in the elliptical central area with a red background. Cutting across them, right in the centre, is the 'DONKERVOORT' name. On the cars, the logo originally sat in the centre of a circular badge, with a blue infill colour, complete with white border.

Donkervoort sports cars may look vaguely familiar and, indeed, Joop Donkervoort was the Dutch agent for Britain's Caterham sports cars before turning his attention to building his own machines. Early Donkervoorts looked very similar to Caterhams – a road car during the week and a racer at the weekend – and, no doubt, there were some sour vibes

shooting across the North Sea in the early 1980s. However, the Donkervoort of today has evolved to become a distinctive marque in its own right, with a large and loyal following.

From Donkervoort's calling on the Technical University in Eindhoven for chassis design expertise to the building of a large new factory in Lelystad in 2000, the cars are Dutch through and through. Apart, that is, from their engines. At first they came from Ford, but since 1995 an agreement with Audi has seen the Audi 1.8T 5V unit under the long bonnet of the current D8, in three states of tune. Today the factory employs thirty staff, who build every one of the fun-filled Donkervoorts by hand.

DUESENBERG

Duesenberg's superb hood ornament, shown on this 1935 Model J Speedster (opposite) that was once owned by Clark Gable, is an Art Deco icon; and its elaborate winged badge is a delightful period piece too.

The dated American expression "it's a duesy" is used to refer to something exceptional; it was the car designs of Fred and August Duesenberg, built in Indianapolis, USA, that gave rise to the phrase. They introduced the first American car with a straight-eight cylinder engine, the Duesenberg Model A, in 1920.

The car's ground-breaking attribute was trumpeted by its badge, carried proudly on the front of its domed radiator cowling, in a shape similar to an open fan. Against the background of a golden American eagle, 'DUESENBERG' sat across the outspread wings, 'STRAIGHT' was below it across the bird's breast, and '8' below that over its claws and tail feathers. All the text was in dark-blue enamel. A temperature gauge for the seven-gallon cooling system sprouted from a large radiator cap, with more feathery, eagle-like wings sticking out either side, and there was a small reproduction of the badge on the instrument's dial.

It was an excellent car, but in 1929

Duesenberg eclipsed it with its Model J – intended as "the world's finest motor car", in the company's own words. The chassis alone cost $8500, half as much again as a Rolls-Royce equivalent, and its 7-litre, straight-eight, twin-camshaft engine, always finished in bright green and gleaming chrome, was closely developed from Duesenberg's racing experience. The Model J was fitted with the most expensive limousine and tourer coachwork then available, and a talented young designer called Gordon Buehrig was hired to co-ordinate and monitor Duesenberg design between the factory and the body-builders. The chassis came with a radiator shell, ready for the body to be fitted, and the badge was now a slimmed-down eagle motif, fitted to the prow of the cowling and bearing just the 'DUESENBERG' name.

Custom-built Model Js, and the phenomenally powerful, supercharged SJ derivative, were owned by millionaires and Hollywood stars ranging from Howard

Hughes and William Randolph Hearst to Greta Garbo and Clark Gable. They looked spectacular, almost dripping with chrome, and in 1931 Buehrig boosted this image with a stylish radiator cap mascot, a two-dimensional streamlined evocation of winged flight that leant forward into the wind and streamed back gracefully along the centre line of the bonnet. It was only an option, but one chosen by many owners of the new and older Model Js. Although it was a fabulous example of Art Deco, it was eclipsed by Buehrig's later work, which included the 1935 Cord 810 – the world's first car whose advanced styling was patented. The magnificent Duesenberg was, however, killed off by bankruptcy in 1937.

FERRARI

Unofficial car industry gossip has it that Ferrari makes more profit from its merchandising operations than it does from either building supercars or dominating the Formula 1 race track. The company staff who spend their time minutely examining Ferrari-branded baseball caps and golf umbrellas for quality are accorded quite some respect in the air-conditioned corridors of the company's Modena HQ.

The story of how a *cavallino rampante*, a prancing black horse, came to be one of the world's most lucrative trademarks is a highly charged one. Enzo Ferrari, born in 1898 near Modena, got a job as an Alfa Romeo team driver when he was twenty-two. Despite a good showing – he came second in the 1922 Mille Miglia – his true skill lay in organization, and by 1929 he was team manager. By 1940 his private company, Auto Avio Costruzione, had built a Fiat-based sports car, and by 1947 the V12 Tipo 125 became the first car to carry the Ferrari (Italian for 'Smith') name.

A legend had, finally, been born.

One of Enzo Ferrari's many female friends, a Countess Paolina Baracca, had had a son, Francesco, a talented pilot who had died in the First World War. He had used the emblem of a rearing horse as his talisman on the side of his aircraft and, despite its unhappy omens, she persuaded Ferrari to use it on his cars in Francesco's honour. It appeared first on the Alfa Romeo team cars entered in the 1932 Spa twenty-four-hour race, but only after Enzo had personally changed the background colour of the shield-shaped design from white to yellow – "this being the colour of Modena", he wrote.

Did Enzo Ferrari embroider this story to add to his own mystique? Some people thought so, but it certainly gave him a presence at Europe's racing circuits in the 1930s, jostling for attention with Maserati's trident and Mercedes-Benz's three-pointed star.

The initials 'SF' were added to the base of the shield, standing for 'Scuderia (Team)

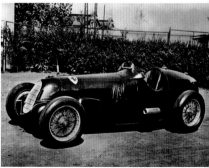

Ferrari never misses a chance to display its talisman on today's cars, with both steering and road wheels prime spots (right and far right); below: the world-famous rectangular badge is part of Pininfarina's beautiful symmetry on the nose of a 1950s Ferrari.

Ferrari', and, complete with a patriotic red, white and green strip across the top, it has been worn by Ferrari racing cars ever since. On Ferrari road cars, however, the horse was given a fuller mane and became the centrepiece of a yellow rectangle. Across the top were the Italian national colours once again, and across the bottom the 'FERRARI' word in a distinctive and legible form, with the top horizontal line of the capital 'F' spanning out across the other letters to meet the corresponding dot atop the 'i'.

Although the horse is often seen as a black silhouette on Ferrari stationery, and as a stand-alone chrome symbol in relief as a grille badge on some road cars, it has remained remarkably true to the First World War original.

Right: the tail of the Ferrari Enzo carries the horse and 'Ferrari' script; far right: Pirelli gets a look in for the tyres but even the brakes are Ferrari-branded on the F430; below and below right: badge and relief emblem add finishing touches to the 612 Scaglietti.

FIAT

Today's Fiat cars carry a badge style that was seen first in 1930 and revived in 1999, at the time of Fiat's one hundreth anniversary; below: the Panda; opposite: the Punto.

The Fabbrica Italiana Automobili Torino (Italian Automobile Factory of Turin) had fitted badges to its cars from the very start. The first spelt out the cumbersome acronym as 'FABBRICA-ITALIANA DI AUTOMOBILI TORINO F I A T' on a flat plate shaped like an unfurled scroll from a treasure chest. It was held in place by two small screws. Its replacement in 1901, however, introduced the 'FIAT' word in prominent block capitals. Its most distinctive feature was a letter 'A' that looked like a capital 'H' with an additional crossbar linking the tops of its two stems, but with the right-hand stem kinked inwards from the centre crossbar to the top to create the 'A'. It meant that the letters could be perfectly spaced, and that the 'A', while quirky, was distinctive.

This 'FIAT' sat in a dark-blue enamel rectangle in the centre of a vista that included vines either side and a sunrise below, while the company's full name was spelt out in a narrow band across the bottom. Two years later the 'FIAT' acronym

in its rectangle was made more prominent in an elliptical badge with a highly decorative Art Nouveau pattern. It was designed by motoring aristocrat Carlo Bicaretti di Ruffia in advance of the first car being sold as a Fiat.

By 1921 the badge had changed to a conventional circular format, with a silver laurel wreath around the edge – no doubt to hint at Fiat's decent performance in Italian races. 'FIAT', complete with its unique 'A', was spelt out in gold-bordered red capitals on a white panel across the central area, a mosaic-pattern stencil strip above and below it. Four years later, the central circle was a plain brown with white 'FIAT' letters, before changing to a dark-blue background in 1929 with silver letters and a thin silver line above and below the acronym.

The colourway changed to red in 1931, at the same time as an alternative emblem for certain Fiat vehicles was used: a tall rectangle with a thick chrome border and, in the centre, 'FIAT' in elongated

Panda

chrome capitals against a rich red enamel panel. Various versions of these two (including a 1959 radiator grille badge resembling an upturned TV screen in a bulgy frame) proliferated until 1966. At that point, the past was swept aside by a 1960s corporate makeover. All Fiat vehicles now carried the 'FIAT' initials in a long parallelogram divided into four equal chrome-bordered sections with a letter in each, on a black (later blue) background.

The 1983 Fiat Uno ushered in a new

badge consisting of five parallel silver lines, sloping slightly to the right on a black background – like the existing badge but with the letters removed and the whole thing squashed together. Fiat's chief designer, Mario Maioli, was inspired by seeing the four giant sections of the existing Fiat logo as a factory roof sign, silhouetted against the sky at dusk – the middle three of the lines being chinks of evening light. Still, it was pretty unemotive, and there were no regrets when, to celebrate its centenary in 1999, Fiat reintroduced a style of badge that had last been seen on one of its cars in 1930. This abrupt about-turn was calculated to haul Fiat back to basics after years of unprofitability; the badge was first displayed on the all-new Fiat Punto, a stylish small family car in the mould of the great Topolino, 600, 127 and Panda models that had gone before it.

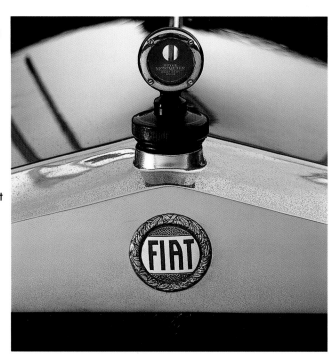

Left: the silver laurel wreath was added to Fiat badges from 1921, hinting at the marque's burgeoning success in motor sport; opposite: arguably Fiat's greatest car ever, the 1957 Nuova 500, put the whole of Italy on four wheels.

Left: the five-bar Fiat logo seen on the 1999 Fiat Multipla and inspired by a roof sign seen at dusk – note the unusual positioning below the windscreen.

FORD

Left: the Model T brought affordable motoring, and mass production, to the world, but initially the cars were identified only by Ford's flowing script on the grille mesh (below). Opposite: the Ford badge has true functionality on the latest Focus.

Ford's script-in-oval trademark has made the company one of the world's top brands, the nineteenth most valuable in 2004, according to *Businessweek* magazine's annual Global Brands Survey. Surprisingly, though, it's had a chequered career as a badge on Ford cars.

The script lettering dates back to the very beginning of the Ford Motor Company's foundation in the summer of 1903. Henry Ford's principal engineering assistant, Childe Harold Wills, had trained as a commercial artist, and in his teens had earned pocket money by printing visiting cards. He still had his old printing press in the attic of his home, and Henry Ford agreed that Wills should use the script typeface that he had employed for his visiting cards to develop a stylized version of the words 'Ford Motor Company' for use on company communications.

This lettering was first used on a car in 1904; it was notable for the curly crossbar on the 'F', strongly redolent of a detail in Coca-Cola's already famous script. On some examples of the Model C, the words 'Ford Motor Company' in the script lettering were used on a brass plate forming part of the starting handle aperture. It was also in 1904 that the script was first used to advertise the cars; it appeared above the windows of Ford's London showroom.

A more developed form of the script appeared on the 1906 Models K and N, which had the four script letters 'Ford' embossed in relief on the radiator header tanks, the letters 'F' and 'd' having long tails. Known widely as the 'script with wings', it was used on all Ford cars up to 1911, when the lettering was revised again in the form still in use today (a few 1910 cars also had a cut-out brass script in this more modern style fixed to the radiator). The script was set inside an oval for dealer insignia in 1912, but the car identification was still the script, by now incorporated into a winged triangle in orange with 'THE UNIVERSAL CAR' below it.

The first car to carry the script-in-oval on

its radiator was the 1927 Model A. The background colour was a deep blue. This oval Ford badge was used on most cars until the end of the 1930s, when it mysteriously vanished, apart from featuring as red script in the chrome bonnet decoration of American models immediately after the Second World War. Perhaps it was seen as plain old-fashioned, particularly after the death of Henry Ford himself in 1947. If the word was seen at all on Ford cars, it was spelt out in separate

Below: the Ford 'script-in-oval' first made its appearance as part of the dealer insignia in 1912, finally arriving at a position on the radiator grille on the Model A in 1927; left: the Ford badge lovingly re-coloured by an owner; far left: for years, anything but the 'blue oval' was used.

Opposite: Ford's V8 was a marketing breakthrough, bringing power and style to the masses; opposite, right: the Ford Focus has been a hit in both Europe and the USA – hard to believe the badge was once absent from most Ford cars for over thirty-five years.

'F-O-R-D' capitals, while individual models such as the Thunderbird, Mustang, Cortina and Falcon bore individual, often elaborate, model insignia.

In 1966 Ford's sprawling global empire, looking for some image consolidation, embarked on a corporate identity programme to give an "easily recognizable and consistent form of identification" to all company dealerships, plants, facilities and even railway rolling stock. The script-in-oval predominated, with a blue-and-white colour scheme. Ford's products were the last to come in for this treatment. In Europe, the Ford oval in chromed plastic with a blue background reappeared on the MkIV Cortina/Taunus in 1976, and within two years graced the front, back and steering wheel of every Ford passenger car. The spread of the oval to every US model was sluggish by comparison, a process not completed until the mid-1980s.

GEELY

This is a badge that few Western drivers or even car industry watchers will be familiar with, but it adorns cars made by what could be the first all-Chinese marque to go global. Of the dozens of Chinese car makers mushrooming in the country's new spirit of business enterprise, Geely shows credible independent promise. This is likely to be boosted by the Chinese government's decree that by 2010 half of all new car sales in this vast emerging market must be in the hands of wholly local firms, and not joint ventures.

So, what of its badge? A blue outer band, edged in chrome on both sides, carries the 'GEELY' name, while an inner light-blue circle has what looks like a white mountain, the peak and right-hand face of which features six incisions that end on the same horizontal plane and diminish progressively in size.

The round shape equates to the earth. "It means we are facing the world and going on the road of internationalization", says Geely. "It contains the meaning that

Geely's career will be stable as a big stone, and will never fall down." The six strokes show sunlight. "Get closer to the sun, and we can absorb more heat. Having experienced competition, we can get more mature", is the rationale. And the sky-blue colour? "It means there will be no end for development."

On 6 November 1986 Geely founder, Li Shufu, made his debut in manufacturing by making refrigerators. By 1992 he had moved into scooters, and the first Geely car was launched in China's Zhejiang Province in August 1998. State approval to become China's first privately owned car maker came in 2001.

That first car was the Merrie, based on a locally made version of the Daihatsu Charade called the Xiali TJ7300. Just two hundred were sold that year, but 2002 saw the Haoqing family car introduced, and in 2003 the Beauty Leopard sports coupé with a 1.3-litre Toyota engine. It made headlines because it came with a karaoke machine as standard equipment. Geely produced

38,888 cars in 2003, of which 32,667 were Haoqings; in April that year, it made its 100,000th car. New models, meanwhile, are being co-developed with Daewoo in South Korea and consultancies Maggiora of Italy and Rücker of Germany.

It's easy to poke fun at Geely's faltering start and unselfconscious mission statements. But how long until Geelys are seen on every street in America and Europe?

GENERAL MOTORS

Right and below right: the acronym stands for General Motors Corporation, and is fitted to a range of mostly commercial vehicles that are a fixture of the US motoring scene; opposite: there is no GM car as such, but the corporate thumbprint often graces cars sold under the company's many brands.

It's the biggest car maker in the world. But there has been only one car actually called a 'General Motors' – the General Motors EV-1, known widely as the GM EV-1. It was a two-seater electric commuter car developed from the 1993 GM Impact concept car and put on sale through Saturn dealers in 1996; several hundred were leased to consumers until the EV-1 was quietly discontinued a few years later.

It was sold as a General Motors vehicle in recognition of its role as a real-life symbol that the corporate entity of GM was taking environmental issues seriously. As a result, its nose bore the General Motors corporate logo, which has hardly ever been carried on the actual metalwork of cars sold under the company's many brands. It's a blue-backed square with a prominent sans serif 'GM' in white at its centre, underscored by a line of equal weight to the text.

General Motors was founded in 1908 as a car-making conglomerate by William Crapo Durant, who used Buick as the 'founder company'. Cadillac, Oldsmobile and Oakland (later renamed Pontiac) were acquired in 1909, followed by Chevrolet in 1910. Britain's Vauxhall was added to the fold in 1925, Germany's Opel in 1928 and Australia's Holden in 1930.

The GM corporate logo was the work of the design team headed by Harley Earl, GM's inspirational founder in 1926 of the company's Paint and Enamel Committee (the world's first dedicated car styling department), which was renamed the Styling Division ten years later. Its exact date of first use on a vehicle is 15 September 1933 when it appeared on the fronts of trucks and buses, although it had been used on radio receivers in 1929.

In contrast to the often flamboyant insignia on General Motors' retail products, the GM logo is sober and blunt, likely to strike the requisite chord with financial institutions by symbolizing mighty power in business-to-business communiqués. Chances to extend its use to cars have been waved aside in the formation of new

marques (such as Saturn in 1985), even though the GMC brand, standing for General Motors Corporation, a colossus of North American trucks and vans, has never possessed anything other than a straightforward text nameplate.

GHIA

Carrozzeria Ghia, a car body-building company, was established in 1919 by Giacinto Ghia, an apprentice coachbuilder with a passion for motoring. By 1935 his workshop in Turin turned out ten handmade car bodies every month, fitted to everything from Fiats to Isotta Fraschinis; many carried a Ghia badge just behind the front mudguard, a bold, chrome outline of the artisan's surname signature.

But during the Second World War Ghia's factory was bombed, and Ghia himself died in February 1944, aged fifty-six. Two designers, Giorgio Alberti and Mario Boano, bought Carrozzeria Ghia's name and goodwill from his widow and set up shop again in 1946. Among the unique car bodies that Ghia built in the 1940s to 1960s were some amazing concept cars and a few roadgoing models for Chrysler, one of which was driven by Sammy Davis Jr. These cars had a new Ghia badge, usually affixed to the bottom of the front wing. It was a red shield with a chrome outline (about the size of a typical key fob) and,

in a diagonal blue band from bottom left to top right, Ghia's chromed signature was respectfully reproduced, the upper bowl of the capital 'G' seemingly breaking out into the red section above. Above this, in a tiny separate casting, a chrome crown with six peaks and a red base added extra majesty.

The most famous car to bear the Ghia name was the cute VW Karmann-Ghia. Ghia styled it, Karmann built it in Germany, and VW, which supplied the Beetle chassis, sold it – shifting 445,000 between 1956 and 1974. On its curvaceous tail was a vibrant, outsize rendering of Ghia's signature scrawled across the sober 'KARMANN' script.

Ford bought Ghia in 1973. It stopped making car bodies and concentrated instead on car styling and prototype-building for its new US master. The enamelled Ghia shield badge was soon slapped on the side of a luxuriously trimmed Ford Mustang II in 1973 in the USA, on a Granada in Europe in 1974, and on a

Mercury Monarch in 1975. There's been a Ghia-liveried version of every mainstream European Ford since, and even the all-new Focus comes with a Ghia trim option. It was all done for kudos, but how many Ford buyers realize today that the tiny badge is actually the moniker of an Italian panelbeater who never even knew what a hatchback was?

CARROZZERIA GHIA TORINO

GORDON KEEBLE

A rare case of irony in car badge design, the tortoise displayed on the beautiful Gordon Keeble GK-1 belied its fire-breathing, Ferrari-baiting performance thanks to its V8 Chevrolet Corvette engine.

Jim Keeble and John Gordon were, respectively, a British engineer and a British financier who believed they could take on Italy's GT supercar makers of the early 1960s and thrash them at their own game. This was partly because they persuaded Italian coachbuilder Bertone to let one of its designers, a young Giorgetto Giugiaro, design a very suave, two-door, four-seater coupé body for them, which was then moulded from glassfibre. It was a glamorous, sexy-looking car that made British equivalents such as the Jensen C-V8 seem extremely passé.

Sitting in Keeble's excellent spaceframe chassis was a fire-breathing Chevrolet Corvette engine, which meant that the 1964 Gordon Keeble GK-1 could hit a heady 135 mph, with Ferrari-eating acceleration to match. Everything about the car was new and fresh – even the photos in its sales brochure were taken by celebrity photographer Terence Donovan.

Its badge was typically enigmatic too. With a sardonic smirk at Ferrari's bucking horse and Maserati's devilish trident, the partners had Gordon Keeble badges made with a simple tortoise image cradled in a laurel wreath.

Sadly, the company did not survive long enough to live out the tortoise-and-hare folk story with its car industry rivals. Gordon Keeble went bust in 1966 after it had made a mere ninety-nine cars in two years. It was a sad end to a promising project – and to one of the few car badges that didn't take itself too seriously.

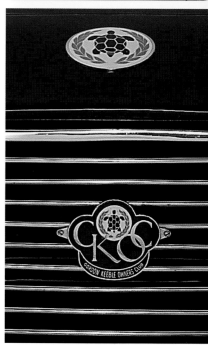

HEULIEZ

The heritage of Heuliez is reflected in its early logo depicting a horse-drawn trap (below) and the latest version (bottom, seen on the Opel Tigra) featuring a cartwheel, but today it's a modern design and engineering business, whose work includes the 1998 Lamborghini-based Pregunta concept (opposite).

There has never actually been a car called a Heuliez, but it's possible you may already know the company's badge without being aware of it. If, that is, you are intimately acquainted with the new Opel/Vauxhall Tigra.

Heuliez is what's known, disparagingly, by the financiers of the City of London as a 'metal-basher', a sub-contract engineering company that usually operates behind the scenes. Adolphe Heuliez was a blacksmith in the country town of Cerizay, on France's western seaboard. When his son Louis succeeded him in the business in the 1920s, he branched out into making English-style horse-drawn traps, and also patented a method of fixing solid rubber tyres to wooden wheels. In 1928 he built a baker's van; a year later his first bus. His son Henri was already running the company by 1950, when Louis died, and had sixty employees. Since then the firm has branched out into coaches, ambulances and contract-built cars.

Its logo was, for many years, the side elevation of a trap in a rectangular frame, showing the shafts and a carriage lamp on a pole at the front. In 1986 this appeared on the B-pillar of a stretched limousine version of the Renault 25, which Heuliez produced on behalf of the French giant. It was absent from Heuliez's most lucrative output, however – estate car versions of the Citroën BX, Xantia and XM.

Today the little power-topped Tigra has taken their place on Heuliez's production lines, and a new Heuliez logo appears on it as a small moulding on the plastic trim surrounding the indicator repeater light on the car's front wings. It consists of a three-dimensional block capital 'H' with the flat image of a cartwheel partly obscured behind it. On paperwork, the 'H' is white and grey, and the wheel green.

HILLMAN

The simplification of the Hillman badge reduced the detailed depiction of three Coventry churches, shown on the Minx below, to the stylized motifs on the badge, bottom; opposite: on this 1969 Hillman Hunter, it was barely recognizable at all.

William Hillman, one of the pillars of Britain's motor industry establishment, hailed from Greenwich, south-east London, but came to Coventry to make bicycles in 1870. He was so successful at it that he was a millionaire twenty years later. He bought himself a country pile, Abingdon House, in Stoke Aldermoor on the edge of the city, and promptly built a car factory in its grounds. From 1907 his speciality was popular small and medium-sized cars.

Hillman's dynasty-building was more impressive than his cars. His two daughters married his joint managing directors, John Black and Spencer Wilks, who went on to head two of Coventry's other famous marques, Standard and Rover respectively.

Hillman owed a lot to Coventry, and he signalled his gratitude in his cars' badge. It incorporated the three spires for which the city was famous, with 'HILLMAN' across them in heavy capital letters. The spires were from St Michael's Cathedral, Christ Church and Holy Trinity Church. In 1928,

after the company was taken over by the Rootes Group, wings (that over-used car industry fallback) were added either side to give the impression of swiftness.

Miraculously, all three spires survived the Blitz (the main buildings of St Michael's and Christ Church were destroyed by Nazi bombs). The 'three spires' theme could still be found on Hillmans right through to the 1960s, progressively becoming more and more abstract to the point that, when it was ousted by the Chrysler logo in 1970, the Hillman badge was an elongated rectangle with what looked like three inverted exclamation marks – minus their full points – on it. No newcomer to the marque could possibly realize that these strokes represented churches.

In 1934 Hillman, by then part of the Rootes Group, introduced the first British car with a radio fitted as standard. It called it the Melody Minx, and it came with a unique chrome radiator mascot featuring a tiny woman whose figure formed part of the frame of a harp.

NMQ 486G

HISPANO-SUIZA

The combined national colours of Spain and Switzerland, together with the magnificent stork mascot, graced many of the finest Hispano-Suizas built up until 1938; the car shown right is a six-cylinder model from 1924, and bodied in tulipwood.

King Alfonso XIII of Spain was rather keen on Hispano-Suizas. He bought his first in 1908 and owned an incredible thirty more of the expensive Barcelona-built machines. He even permitted the company to name a car after him. Yet the marque's name, Hispano-Suiza, means 'Spanish-Swiss'. This was because the engineering genius behind the cars was Marc Birkigt. Born in 1878 in Switzerland, and a gifted electrical engineer, he first proved his worth designing a power station and electric trains for Spanish entrepreneur Emilio La Caudra. When La Caudra decided to enter the car market in 1904, he honoured his protégé in the car's title.

He also honoured him in the car's badge. The focal point was a wheel with voluminously plumed wings sprouting from either side, but behind this was a larger circle featuring, above the wheel, the red/yellow/red stripes of the Spanish flag and, below the wheel, the white cross on a red background of the Swiss one.

Hispano-Suizas soon became some of the most sought-after luxury cars in Europe, and to meet this demand the company opened a plant in Paris in 1911, so that, bizarrely, a car called a 'Spanish-Swiss' was now also French-built. In 1931, during the Depression, the satellite plant gave birth to the incredible Type 68 V12. By 1938, however, car manufacture had ceased as both parts of Hispano-Suiza slid into nationalized control and concentrated on defence and aerospace work.

Like that of Rolls-Royce and Duesenberg, Hispano-Suiza's badge is overshadowed by its radiator mascot. It's a magnificent evocation of a stork in flight, fixed to the car by its wing tips in their lowest position in the flapping cycle. First appearing on the H6 model in 1919, it was the product of sculptor François Victor Bazin working from a rough three-dimensional model made by Louis Massuger, a test engineer at the Paris plant. He got the idea for it when the name of the street on which the factory was situated was changed to rue du Capitaine

Guynemer, honouring a fearless French First World War pilot. Georges Guynemer's plane carried a stork motif as a lucky talisman (France was campaigning to regain control of the German-annexed Alsace region, where storks bred in large numbers) and was powered by a Hispano-Suiza V8 engine. He crashed in September 1917 while on a sortie.

This potent symbol of French freedom was also fitted to Spanish-built Hispano-Suizas, further complicating the imagery.

HOLDEN

Opposite: the earliest Holden of 1948 was Australia's first indigenous car design; more recent models have included the Commodore (below), and Barina (bottom), but all have retained variations of Holden's trademark lion rolling a stone.

Australia's Holden has a weird background, and a pretty strange badge too. Holden & Frost started as a firm of saddle- and cart-makers before turning to fabricating truck bodies. In 1928 it became an assembler of British and US General Motors cars for the local market, and in 1931 GM took control of the company, renaming it General Motors-Holden's Ltd.

Until 1928, Holden's rudimentary trademark had depicted a man with wings, holding a car and posed against the background of a factory. But after that date all Holden-built vehicles sported a new nameplate showing a lion sitting up and pushing a rough-hewn circular stone with his front paw. It was designed by Australian sculptor George Rayner Hoff.

There were two influences. First, legend had it that the whole concept of the wheel came about after an Egyptian lion was seen rolling a stone. Secondly, a lion had been used as the motif for the 1924 Wembley Exhibition in London, a celebration of the British empire that had

naturally been a big talking point 'down under'.

The first proper Holden car was launched in 1948, although its development was actually against the wishes of General Motors; it was sponsored by the Australian government in partnership with Holden's managing director, Laurence Hartnett, both to create a car suited to Australian roads and also to stem the outflow of currency.

It had the lion badge affixed to the centre of its chrome grille, although it was now shown at the foot of an obelisk in a badge shaped like an inverted shield. Since then, Holden has continued to build a mixed stable of its own designs and other GM cars. In 1972, the badge was changed to an elegant cut-out of the lion and its plaything, and in 1994 a new version was enclosed in a double-rimmed circle. It is generally silver on cars and red and white on communications.

HONDA

HONDA

Honda's 'H' logos have stuck to the same theme since 1962; the first four-wheeled Honda, the T360 truck (bottom) had a giant logo pressed into its bonnet, which was toned down for the N600 (below); the recent Civic Type-R (opposite) sports an extremely prominent badge.

In 1962 a brand new marque burst on to the motoring scene, although Honda was already familiar to much of the world's motorbike-riding community. Since then, Honda has become an absolute byword for consistency, not just in the excellence of its build quality and reliability but also in the application of its badges.

Honda's first two vehicles, announced concurrently in October 1962, were an odd couple: the S360 was a pretty two-seater roadster, while the T360 was a tiny pick-up truck. Although Soichiro Honda's heart lay in sports cars, in his head he knew the pick-up would be a strong seller in booming 1960s Japan.

Honda's successful motorbikes had long carried a flying feather motif; Honda cars, however, took the capital letter 'H' and gave it a rounded look, splaying the two stems outwards and smoothing the crossbar into them. The T360 had a huge rendition of this pressed into its stubby bonnet, with 'HONDA' across it in red – the largest Honda logo ever seen on a

vehicle. The S360, by contrast, had a more seemly silver 'H' in a red square on its bonnet, seen later as a red 'H' in a black rectangle as a grille badge and a chrome cut-out 'H' as a wing side badge on the similar S800.

Since then the 'H' has been widened, lengthened and used with and without a frame. It's sometimes been seen against a red background, in silver or white, and today is mostly encountered as a framed, chrome cut-out on new Hondas. Essentially, however, it is still the same design.

Honda is also choosy about where its badge is used. Both the Land Rover Discovery and Isuzu Amigo have been sold with Honda badges, as the Honda Crossroad and Honda Passport respectively … but only as interim models while Honda developed its own 4x4 range that met its rigorous quality standards.

HOOPER

Rather than a badge, Hooper-bodied cars were identified by this plate (left) fixed to the door well – discretion was paramount; in the 1930s, the company was at the centre of London's historic coachbuilding industry (opposite), and after the Second World War it continued to turn out imposing cars such as this Daimler DE36 limousine (below).

A bodymaker rather than a manufacturer, Hooper is a fairly obscure company, despite being founded in 1807 and having connections with the British royal family dating back to the reign of William IV. However, in the sixty years between 1899 and 1959, Hooper & Co. created some of the most expensive and imposing limousine bodies ever seen. They were invariably fitted to Daimler or Rolls-Royce chassis and were supplied, complete with whatever eccentric or sybaritic features they demanded, to potentates and tycoons worldwide. A few Hooper body styles were ugly, but most were restrained and elegantly British.

The company was rejuvenated in the mid-1980s, when it offered modified versions of contemporary Rolls-Royces and Bentleys. It also acquired the Metrocab London taxi business, renaming it Hooper Metrocab.

However, in contrast to Italian and French coachbuilders, firms such as Hooper – beholden as they were to the suppliers of their chassis such as Rolls-Royce – were uneasy and reticent about their identity.

A Hooper badge or crest was rarely, if ever, fitted to a car's exterior: to discover who had made the bodywork, you would have to open a driver or passenger door and there, discreetly screwed to the door frame, was a long metal plate with 'HOOPER & CO. (COACHBUILDERS) LTD. LONDON' inscribed upon it. Such artisanal discretion seems very strange in today's designer-orientated world, especially as clients would specifically seek out Hooper on the basis of its creative skills and fastidiousness.

Hooper did devise a badge in the 1980s, a capital 'H' in a plain shield with the simplest of wing details added to the top. As far as I can ascertain, it was only ever fitted to the Metrocab, surely among the ugliest vehicles on London's roads today.

So Hooper's is one of the greatest badges that never was.

HUDSON

Hudson cars were financed by a department store tycoon but adopted the ship imagery of an eponymous seventeenth-century adventurer; the models shown here are both Hudson Commodores, c 1955 car (below) and a 1951 model (opposite).

Hudson is today described as a 'Chrysler heritage brand'; it's a handy euphemism for a marque that was last seen on a new car in 1957. Founded in 1909, the first model was the work of designer Howard Coffin, but as his surname would hardly be appropriate for its radiator badge, the car was called a Hudson after Joseph L. Hudson, a New York department store owner who provided much of the finance for the venture.

Hudson introduced a six-cylinder model in 1912, and two years later claimed to be the planet's biggest manufacturer of six-cylinder cars. The king of NYC haberdashery soon saw his name on the polished brass radiator cowling of the cars. Hudson used a white triangle and the words 'HUDSON', 'SUPER' and 'SIX' stacked in descending order down towards the triangle's point at the bottom; tucked into the acute-angled tip was the information 'REG. U.S. PATENT OFF'.

The badge changed with the advent of the first Hudson straight-eight in the 1930s.

Two white triangles in what looked like a huge pen nib remained a centrepiece on a red, pendant-shaped background, with 'HUD' and 'SON' split by its lower tip. At the top, either side of the triangle, were two stylized castle turrets as symbols of the Hudson's ruggedness, and below them two mirror-image ships as symbols of the adventurous lifestyle that a Hudson could bring its owner. Despite the retail background to the Hudson name, these ships were images of the *Half Moon*, sailed to America by the Dutch-backed English adventurer Henry Hudson in the seventeenth century. This reflected the great US interest in revivalism at the time.

Despite launching the novel and extremely stylish 'step-down' range in 1948, Hudson was too underfinanced to compete with Ford and General Motors. In 1954 it merged with Nash to form American Motors Corporation, and all Hudsons became Ramblers three years later.

HYUNDAI

Now the seventh largest car maker in the world, Hyundai was once a purveyor of truly anonymous cars. Between around 1987 and 1991, its Pony, Stellar and Sonata models didn't have a badge at all, the best that could be found in terms of identity being the word 'HYUNDAI' in pseudo-electronic text as a plastic add-on to the boot or radiator grille.

Originally, however, there had been a badge on the Pony, a small family saloon introduced in 1976 and the first car created from scratch by the South Korean conglomerate Hyundai. It took the form of a black rectangle with a capital 'H' together with a 'D' represented by an infilled outline. A speeding horse in red was also sometimes encountered on documents relating to the car, for which much of the backing and engineering know-how came from the UK (but engines from Japan's Mitsubishi), but it never galloped its way on to a bonnet or steering wheel.

In 1991 a new logo was introduced, which has remained on all Hyundai cars (apart from the XG luxury saloon) as a chrome cut-out badge to this day. Superficially, it looks like a fluidly expressed 'H' embraced by an oval frame, but there is a dual meaning: it's meant to represent two people linking arms, a graphic reassurance, Hyundai says, of the relationship between the company and its customers.

The badge sits particularly comfortably on the Hyundai Santa Fe and Tucson, two SUVs that with their curvaceous styling are anything but anonymous. Hyundai is aiming for a place among the world's top five car makers by 2010; bearing in mind that it sold just over 100,000 cars in 1979 but 1.9 million in 2003, that could easily happen.

INFINITI

Nissan hopes its Infiniti brand will go on for ever, and the positive reception the US-only marque has received since 1990, with cars such as the latest Q45 seen here, seems to assure that; before long, the Infiniti badge will be familiar in Europe too.

Nissan established its Infiniti marque as a US-only upmarket brand in 1990, hoping to use it to push into new market sectors well above the humdrum saloons that it had mostly produced up to that point. It was a move mirrored by Toyota with its Lexus.

At the forefront of this Nissan venture was the all-new Infiniti Q45, an imposing saloon powered by a 4.5-litre V8 engine and with an aura of luxury that pitted it against desirable imports from Mercedes-Benz and Jaguar. A new marque meant a new logo, and Nissan went for an elliptical device in heavy chrome. However, the curved line of the outline shape, carried round from above, jutted up into a triangular pinnacle, with the chrome line tapering to a pin-sharp point – that is, of course, disappearing to infinity.

This motif had an uncharacteristically fussy application on the Q45, as it was mounted on a curvaceous, four-sided frame, its background festooned with intricate scroll decoration. However, on other Infiniti models, which were essentially rebranded Nissans anyway, the motif was carried as a plain chrome cut-out mounted on the radiator grille. The G20 had the smallest variant, as it was also the closest to a standard Nissan – the car was all but identical to Europe's Primera.

By 1994 the Q45 had received a handsome new chrome grille with a much toned-down badge. Ever since, however, Infiniti cars have worn their logo with increasing prominence: the latest M45, Q45 and FX45 – Infiniti's bold take on a sporty SUV – wear it as the centrepiece of a boldly slatted chrome grille, which Infiniti calls a 'waterfall'.

The Infiniti badge looks set to become very familiar. Nissan, under guidance from its masters at majority shareholder Renault, has begun a global roll-out of Infiniti, starting in South Korea and expected in Europe by 2008. Who knows if it can establish itself as a bona fide prestige marque in the Mercedes-Benz mould?

INVICTA

The Invicta S1 (opposite and bottom) revives a marque last seen in 1950 but whose glory days were in the late 1920s and early 1930s when 'low-chassis' models such as this 4.5-litre car (below) were sportsmen's favourites.

This is another British sporting marque that might have been forgotten, except among well-informed enthusiasts, but for the fact that the name was revived on an exciting new sports car, the S1, in 2002 – the first time an Invicta had featured in new car price guides since 1950. The S1 is a high-performance two-seater, with power from a 4.6-litre Ford Mustang V8 engine and the distinction of being the first production car with a body made totally from carbon-fibre composite material, widely used in the racing car world for its strength and lightness.

On its sleek nose is another revival – the Invicta badge last seen in 1933. In the centre, the prominent shape of a chrome capital 'I' carries the 'INVICTA' word, with each black letter stacked vertically down its stem. Billowing out either side are well-plumed ornithological wings, each feather originating in green and turning to blue before ending in red at its tip. In enamel rather than plastic, this badge had been seen on the radiator surrounds

of Invicta's classic models such as the rakish, 100 mph S-type, the winner of the 1931 Monte Carlo Rally driven by Donald Healey (later to found Austin-Healey). Some Invictas have also sported a prominent metal cut-out of the capital 'I' attached to the radiator grille mesh.

Between 1925 and 1930, however, Invictas had carried an altogether plainer badge: a rectangle with its corners given scalloped, quarter-circle indentations and 'INVICTA' in black-enamelled, block letters framed elegantly within. It looked more like the brass plate attached to the wall of an old-established solicitor than a radiator badge, but there was no mistaking it for any other car of the vintage period. Used on the shortlived Invicta Black Prince luxury car of 1946–50, it is also embossed on the leather seats of the new S1 – a clever reference to Invicta's rich heritage.

ISOTTA FRASCHINI

Isotta Fraschini cars, with their ground-breaking straight-eight engines (right) were among the most sought-after cars of the 1920s and 1930s; right, below: the company's radiator mascot was stunning, its radiator badge elegant; opposite: the ill-fated revival of Isotta Fraschini in 1996, an intriguing 'what if...'.

Isotta Fraschini was an august Italian manufacturer of luxury cars that, in 1906, was the second biggest car maker in the country, turning out three hundred cars to Fiat's eighteen hundred – not exactly Henry Ford territory, but still impressive for the day. Nonetheless, the company – co-founded in 1900 by wealthy lawyer Cesare Isotta and the car enthusiast brothers Oreste and Vincenzo Fraschini – made some impressive, racing-orientated machines up to the First World War, their 1913 racing cars being the first in the world with brakes on all four wheels.

After the war, the firm switched to large luxury cars, introducing the Tipo 8 in 1918 as the world's first car with a series-produced straight-eight engine. In 1924 came the even more powerful Tipo 8A. One of these, finished in two-tone purple, became the first car ever to be used by the pope after the people of Milan presented it as a gift to Pius XI in 1928. Thereafter, though, it was downhill all the way – car production fizzled out in the 1930s as the

firm became involved in aero and marine engines.

Up to the arrival of the 8A, Isottas had carried the straightforward identity of a domed circular badge with the 'IF' initials in white against a dark-blue background in the middle portion. Around the edge, a dark-blue band held the curved 'ISOTTA FRASCHINI' at the top and 'MILANO' at the bottom, separated by two five-pointed stars. The 8A, however, had an upright rectangular badge, in which 'IF' was set off by a dark-blue square in the centre, with the words 'Isotta' and 'Fraschini' stacked above in florid, interwoven script. In the space below the square was inscribed 'MILANO'.

Revivals of Isotta Fraschini cars were attempted in 1947 and 1996, but both proved abortive.

Isuzu's breakthrough ca
was the well-liked Bellet
(below), but today the
company specializes in
SUVs and pick-ups such
as the Rodeo; opposite
the vehicles don't wear
badge at all, making
do only with an 'ISUZU'
nameplate.

The heat of competition in the global car industry is intense; it proved too much for Japan's Isuzu in 1993 when it decided to quit passenger car manufacture and stick to trucks, pick-ups and 4x4 vehicles like the Vehi-Cross. Its 1-ton D-Max pick-up is the fifth in a series stretching back thirty-one years. Generally these do not carry a logo, making do with the 'ISUZU' text displayed prominently on grille, bodysides and tailgate.

The first vehicle to carry the Isuzu name arrived in 1934 when the Ishikawajima Automotive Works, which previously assembled British Wolseley cars under licence, launched a truck named after the Isuzu river. This flows past Japan's oldest shrine, the Grand Shrine of Ise, and was saluted by the appropriate Japanese characters in a roughly ovular, upright badge with an organic, knobbly edge.

Ishikawajima underwent several mergers until Isuzu Motors Ltd was officially established in 1949, by which time it was Japan's leading diesel engine maker. It returned to cars in 1953 by building the Hillman Minx under licence from Britain's Rootes Group; once it had got the knack of modern car making, it launched its first independent design, the Bellel, in 1961, complete with the Grand Shrine of Ise symbol on its bonnet, although the smaller Bellet of 1963 was a more accomplished effort.

In July 1971 Isuzu signed an agreement with General Motors Corporation that gave the US giant a one-third share in the company (it has since been as high as 49% but is today 12%) and paved the way for Isuzu exports to the USA. Isuzu also built its own version of GM's 'T Car' project, called the Isuzu Gemini. For this the existing Japanese logo was deemed too parochial, and Isuzu devised a new one as a square red badge on the car. In the centre was a white symbol divided down its centre, with both mirror-image 'pillars' tapering to a point. According to Isuzu, these represent "corporate and societal growth against the sunburst red

background, (reflecting) the company's determination to meet the needs of the age". Underscoring them was 'ISUZU' in white.

Although still widely used on communications (and recently made free-standing with what appears to be a casually drawn circle surrounding it), the logo vanished from Isuzu cars as the 1990s dawned.

JAGUAR

You enjoy
a very special kind of motoring
—when you own a Jaguar

That powerful and graceful feline from South America, the jaguar, encapsulates the virtues of Jaguar cars. Which, of course, is exactly why company founder William Lyons chose the model name in 1935 for his new range of SS cars. SS Cars Ltd clearly had the wrong ring to it, so in 1945 it was replaced by Jaguar Cars Ltd (although the canny Mr Lyons had registered the name as far back as 1938, just in case).

Its dominant logo, known internally at Jaguar since the 1980s as 'the leaper', derives from a profile view of a pouncing jaguar mascot, which first appeared in 1938. Prior to that, only a winged 'SS Jaguar' emblem identified the cars; it was a private accessory manufacturer, Desmo, that filled the gap with a radiator mascot. Apparently, William Lyons was appalled with this tacky caricature, saying it looked like "a cat that had been shot off a fence". He engaged his then PR man Bill Rankin, an enthusiastic amateur sculptor, to design "an anatomically correct" version, which was artfully refined by motoring artist (and keen SS owner) Frederick Gordon Crosby.

It was announced as the official Jaguar mascot, priced at two guineas, late in 1938. Still in production today for export markets where safety legislation allows it to be fitted, 'the leaper' is substantially as it appeared in the 1930s, although about eight centimetres shorter and with the animal in mid-leap rather than just leaving the ground as it was depicted originally.

Based on this masterwork, subsequent Jaguars have also carried a wide variety of two-dimensional jaguar symbols. The Jaguar MkV–IX saloons carried a badge on the prow of their radiator shells in the old SS style, a flattened hexagonal outline closely tracing the 'JAGUAR' name in the centre and flanked by rather predictable, if fulsomely detailed, wings. The XK sports cars and MkI/II saloons then switched to circular bonnet badges, both cast/enamelled and later clear-view plastic and in a variety of colourways, depicting the fearsome, toothy frontal view of a growling jaguar as a centrepiece, and

then usually an outer ring carrying such messages as 'JAGUAR CARS LTD', 'XK150', '3.4-LITRE' or 'E-TYPE'. One unusual XK150 badge does away with the central feline face altogether to make way for a list of Jaguar's five Le Mans victories in the 1950s.

After featuring what looked like a circular bronze relief of the jaguar's face for the 1975–94 XJS, Jaguar returned to the 1950s/1960s sports car theme for its XK8 and XKR sports cars, adding to the huge number of existing variations with new engine descriptions such as '4-LITRE' and 'SUPERCHARGED'. Saloons since the 1979 XJ Series III have carried a more subtle badge, the jaguar's face, initially on a black shield, reproduced small and sitting at the very prow of the radiator grille. On the latest XJ range, the animal's head is in stand-alone chrome relief.

Another badge, applied to the wing sides of saloon models such as the Series I–III XJ6, features an outline side profile of 'the leaper' in mid-bound. This has also been used widely on literature, dealership

insignia, corporate items and licensed products in black, white, green and silver. It is most frequently seen as an overhead addition to Jaguar's simple and elegant corporate typescript.

One way or another, the message of feline grace and power has been communicated via Jaguar badges loud and clear for over sixty years.

Jeep

JEEP

This logo (left) sometimes made an appearance on Jeep vehicles, but certainly never on the war-time Willys (right, top).

The basic Jeep nameplate (right, bottom) was adopted for car flanks in 1975, was occasionally seen as a chintzy bonnet ornament (right, centre), and finally made it to the front of a car on the 1984 Cherokee (opposite).

Among text-only car logos – and there aren't many – Jeep's is surely the most instantly recognizable in the world. The four letters of 'Jeep' are seen as a black-based, silver-fronted plastic nameplate on the nose of the current Jeep Liberty/Cherokee and Grand Cherokee, situated above the trademark heavy, vertically slatted air intake. The font, which is Franklin Gothic, has the clarity of a child's early reading book, or maybe signage at a hospital. The lack of stylization is highly unusual.

Jeep's very lack of a logo is rooted in its origins as a four-wheel-drive military vehicle in the Second World War. As production at Willys-Overland's factory in Ohio rose in 1942, the name Jeep became synonymous with it; it was spoken military shorthand for 'GP', the abbreviation for 'general purpose', but it's also thought that a popular contemporary newspaper cartoon character called 'Eugene the Jeep' played a part in making Jeep a universal word. There was no 'trademark': the Jeep was conceived purely for the theatre of war. However, Willys-Overland fought a legal battle to register it as its own trademark in 1950, and subsequently proceeded to market its 4x4 products to civilian customers with great success.

Soon afterwards, the company began to stamp 'J-e-e-p' in outsize letters into the tailgate panels of its pick-ups, in an earlier text style with a drop-capital 'J' and serifs. The change to today's style came in 1975, when the nameplate was fitted to the front wings of the basic Jeep CJ, and not at all on the larger, four-door Wagoneer. It was the 1984 Cherokee, Jeep's smaller sport-utility car and the first with integral construction rather than a separate chassis frame, that the Jeep name – so redolent of American military might and the great outdoors – finally made it to the prow of the bonnet. In written communications for the marque, which is now part of DaimlerChrysler, 'Jeep' is always accompanied by the '®' symbol huddled beside the descender of the 'p' – an illustration of how closely it is guarded.

JENSEN

The Jensen 541 (below) and CV-8 (bottom and opposite) were Jensen's staple products in the 1950s and 1960s respectively, their badges differing only in the enamel colours; the man in the main picture is actor Steve Forrest in the role of 1960s TV crime-solver *The Baron*.

Jensen introduced its first car in 1936 after several years as a well-respected coachbuilder. In 1976 it was declared insolvent; this perennial 'creaking gate' of the British car industry finally fell off its hinges for good in 2002, after yet another failed attempt to resurrect the marque – the S-V8 sports car that vanished after just twenty had been made.

That 1936 Jensen, the elegant S-type, introduced Jensen's badge, yet another variation on the winged theme with three sharply pointed, feathery sections sticking out each side, the top one with the widest span; it was supposed to summon up the image of a falcon, and so suggest speed. Bang in the middle of this chromed extravaganza, a gold-enamelled disc carried the 'JENSEN' name diagonally from bottom right to top left, with the serifs of the two 'N's and the crossbar of the 'J' distinctively elongated and tapered for further visual motion.

Red enamel replaced gold for the 1955 541, yellow appeared on the 1958 541R,

and it was back to red for the later 541S and C-V8. But for the Interceptor of 1966 the device was reduced in size, narrowed and set against a thin, four-sided lozenge with a dark-red background. The shape was the same, but feathers were now suggested at the top and bottom, while 'JENSEN' was spelt out in slightly flattened black capitals across the centre, underlined in the same text weight. The final 1970s Interceptors carried an additional badge, a black-enamelled (very occasionally red) shield topped with a crown and showing a long capital 'J' in the centre. It was fitted to C-pillars on J series saloons and the rear edge of the boot lid on convertibles.

The Jensen-Healey was the company's shortlived small sports car, made between 1972 and 1976. Its badge was a black-on-chrome rectangle filled almost to its edges with a prominent capital 'H'. Between the two stems, 'JENSEN' was placed above the crossbar and 'HEALEY' below it. Dull, for sure, but highly legible.

KARMANN

The voluptuous Volkswagen Karmann-Ghia (opposite) is the most famous creation of the venerable German coachbuilder; it featured this mid-period badge, another version of which, with a spoked wheel instead of the Ghia insignia, adorned the Volkswagen Beetle cabriolet.

Few coachbuilders survived the difficult transition from horse-drawn carriages to today's high-technology motor industry, but Germany's Karmann did, and is flourishing as never before. As well as continuing its traditional role as designer and manufacturer of convertible versions of cars, such as the Audi A4 and Mercedes-Benz CLK, it acts as a contract developer of niche models, such as Chrysler's Crossfire.

Karmann came to worldwide prominence as the originator of the Volkswagen Beetle cabriolet, which led to the Karmann-Ghia coupé and later soft-top editions of the VW Golf and Ford Escort, but the company has its roots in the Christian Klages carriage business in Osnabrück, which Wilhelm Karmann acquired in 1901. Five years later he changed its name to Wagenfabrik Wilhelm Karmann, and began fitting a wheel hubcap to its stylish horse-drawn vehicles bearing the 'Karmann' signature underlined with an extension of the final 'n' and with 'OSNABRÜCK' beneath it.

Karmann had moved seamlessly into making car bodies by the 1920s, and until 1955 cars carrying its coachwork – including several Adler convertibles, the Ford Eifel roadster, the Volkswagen Beetle cabriolet and Ford Taunus station wagon – bore a rectangular badge with the name 'Karmann Karosserie'. This featured a single outsize 'K' to start both words, the leg of which also originated the underscore, in place of the 'n' of the old nameplate.

In the mid-1960s a replacement badge was added to the Beetle cabriolet and Karmann-Ghia sports car, on the left-hand side front wing below the A-pillar: a lateral, quasi-elliptical emblem with the 'KARMANN' name surmounted by a spoked wheel – an element taken from the local Osnabrück coat of arms. Beginning with the Volkswagen Scirocco coupé in 1974, and also on the Volkswagen Golf cabriolet in 1979, the 'KARMANN' name transferred to a rectangular nameplate with the Osnabrück wheel on the left of it on the same level.

In 1990 a new era began for Karmann when it was contracted to build the Renault 19 cabriolet. For this, the German company's own design studio created a new shield-shaped badge that was fitted to the bodyside aspect of the car's folding hood cover. The keynote colour was dark blue, in the centre of which was the Osnabrück wheel in peep-through chrome. At the top, a red band was given three six-pointed chrome stars, while a blue band below that carried the 'KARMANN' name in yellow underlined capitals.

It was subsequently fitted to the Megane cabriolet (lower down, beside the rear wheel arch) and Golf III cabriolet (on the roll-bar pillar). These days, however, Karmann's clients generally insist on little or no Karmann identity, so the shield has most recently appeared on concept show cars such as the Karmann Transformer of 2001. The latest Renault Megane II CC has no emblem, but a 'KARMANN' name pressed discreetly into its bodywork.

KIA

Kia was founded in South Korea in 1944 to make metal tubes. Although Kia was an unknown marque in 1991, its first car was familiar: the Kia Pride was actually the previous-generation Mazda 121 re-badged. This humble little car had been co-developed by Mazda and Ford with the bargain basement of the US market in mind, where it was sold from 1987 as the Ford Festiva. To reduce costs, the cheap labour of South Korea's Kia Motors was contracted to assemble it. The novel US-Japan-Korea protocol eventually allowed Kia to export the Festiva/Pride on its own terms. However, perhaps still under the yoke of being a 'contractor', the Pride's plastic chrome-on-black badge was the 'Kia' name depicted to resemble a smokestack factory, the left-hand stem of the 'K' as the chimney, with the dot of the 'i' and the upper loop of the 'a' billowing fumes.

The Pride built up a reputation for reliability, and Kia quickly capitalized on this by adding the Mentor family car and

Sportage off-roader to its line-up in 1994. The Kia factory emblem briefly appeared in a maroon oval surround on the Mentor, but it was soon replaced. Now the oval was chrome-bordered with a red background and the three chrome letters of 'KIA' set centrally. The sole distinctive touch was the lack of a crossbar on the 'A'.

Crippling economic conditions in South Korea in 1998 scuppered Kia's rise, and it was rescued from insolvency by rival Hyundai. All new Kia models since 2001 have shared platforms with equivalent Hyundais, and the company has scored critical hits with the Picanto city car and Sorento 4x4. The cars have begun to sport a beefed-up badge with thicker chrome and a dark-grey background.

LADA

You might be forgiven for thinking that Togliatti doesn't sound very Russian. That's not surprising: the site of this immense car factory, six hundred miles south-east of Moscow, was renamed to honour Palmiro Togliatti, the then chairman of the Italian Communist Party who helped establish the Volszhkji Avtomobilnji Zavod (VAZ, or Volzhsky Motor Works) with Fiat in 1966.

It took three years to build the plant on one thousand acres of grassy plains beside the Volga river. There are over ninety miles of automated assembly lines; thirteen giant machine shops produce 500 tons of metal castings and 180 tons of forgings daily; and over 750,000 cars are built annually. Unlike most manufacturers, almost everything in a Lada is made at this single vast site.

Togliatti produced its first car in 1970, based closely on the design of the Fiat 124 and called the VAZ 2101, Zhiguli or Lada for export. Over twelve million of these have since been made and, much updated, it's still churned out today as the Lada Riva. Combined with the Fiat 124, it's the third best-selling single model design of all time, after the Volkswagen Beetle and Ford Model T.

All early cars had an upright, shield-shaped emblem showing, in chrome on a black background, the front of a Viking longship. (Vikings once invaded the local area – an odd thing to commemorate.) It was in side profile, with figurehead and sail easily identifiable, but not similar enough to Rover's to cause any apparent discord.

Subsequent Lada models, such as the four-wheel drive Niva – the factory's first independent design – in 1978, and the Samara front-wheel drive hatchback of 1986, had the same badge. However, in 1995 VAZ began making the 110, 111 and 112 models, which were relatively modern saloons and estates in the Ford Mondeo idiom (they are now sold as Ladas in Russia too). Simultaneously, it updated the badge, turning it into a flattened ellipse but keeping the longboat image compressed rather uncomfortably at its centre. On some small models, it's seen as a chrome outline through which the body colour is visible.

Add a Lada to your life.

LAGONDA

The Lagonda badge had many variations (left) but in 1931 it adopted the winged imagery so beloved of sports car manufacturers; opposit and below: the early rendition of that badge on the imposing, cowle radiator shell of a 1930s M45 sports tourer.

Although Lagonda is a celebrated British marque, it was founded by an American consulting engineer, Wilbur Gunn. He settled in Staines, Middlesex, England, in 1891, where he built a motorcycle at home. He called it a Lagonda, the Shawnee Indian word for Buck's Creek in his native Springfield, Ohio. Motorbikes led to three-wheeled cars and a four-wheeler in 1908.

Gunn had ambitions to be England's answer to Henry Ford with small popular cars. But after the Second World War, and his death in 1920, Lagonda concentrated on sporting cars. They still bore Gunn's Lagonda badge, originally a pressing into the radiator header tank and then a brass plate, as a white, enamelled oval with a thin band of blue around the edge and 'Lagonda' in the centre, again in blue, in an elegant, flowing, almost italicized script. The stem of the capital 'L' looped around to underline the word and attach itself to the finial of the final letter 'a', interrupted by the curled descender of the 'g'. A further flourish came from an elongated

triangular device spanning out from the top of the 'L'.

Lagonda 2- and 3-litre cars came with a long rectangular badge, curving at the ends around its fixing screws. 'LAGONDA' featured an outsize 'L' and final letter 'A', while small semi-circular bulges in the centre emphasized the words 'STAINES' and 'ENGLAND', cradled as though seen through a magnifying glass. It was dark blue with white lettering.

The badge underwent a total redesign in 1931. It used the commonplace concept of the outstretched feathers of a bird, but with its wing tips upswept. A central section, in dark blue to contrast with the copper-coloured feathers, looked like London Underground's station motif, a circle with a bar running through it. On this, 'LAGONDA' was spelt out, the crossbars to the 'A's triangulated downwards. It adorned some of Lagonda's most sensational models including, from 1937, its V12s.

In 1947 Lagonda was acquired by industrialist David Brown and merged with

Aston Martin. For a new 2.6-litre model, the 'A's were normalized and the Lagonda badge was changed to red on chrome with white enamel for the feathers. He added 'DAVID' and 'BROWN' to the top two feathers immediately above 'LAGONDA'.

Lagonda was revived in 1976 with the Aston Martin Lagonda, a sensational wedge-shaped saloon. 'DAVID BROWN' was deleted. The Lagonda name (now Ford-owned) has been dormant since a prototype, the Vignale, was shown in 1993

LAMBORGHINI

For all its rich heritage, Lamborghini has one of the least adulterated badge stories of all. The iconic Lamborghini badge was first fitted to a pulse-racing car in 1962 and, forty-three years later, it still adorns some of the most exciting sports cars in the world in an almost identical form.

Legend has it that Ferruccio Lamborghini, a millionaire through his involvement in making tractors and heating equipment, was incensed at his treatment by Enzo Ferrari. Lamborghini had owned four Ferraris when he complained to Mr Ferrari that the cars were not up to his hard-driving style. Ferrari is supposed to have told him to stick to tractors, at which point Lamborghini resolved to build his own supercar to better anything Ferrari could come up with. Well, that's the story, anyway; it is more likely that a shrewd businessman like Lamborghini turned to making a supercar after his application to the Italian government to become a helicopter manufacturer was turned down.

He set about hiring the cream of Italy's engineering and design talent and, in 1962, presented the Lamborghini 350GT, a sleek and beautiful V12 sports car. For its bonnet badge, Lamborghini chose a raging, hoof-scraping, fighting bull with its head lowered in the ready-to-charge position. A front three-quarter image of this in gold was placed in a black, chrome-edged shield with 'LAMBORGHINI' ranged around the shield's gently curved top. In fact the badge had existed before the car, as Ferruccio Lamborghini, born under the star sign Taurus, had already used it on his tractor range. It was merely a happy coincidence that it was an even more combative, virile image than Ferrari's own bucking stallion.

The 1966 Miura (named after Antonio Miura, a famous Spanish breeder of fighting bulls) was a glorious, mid-engined supercar, but even that was topped by Lamborghini's masterpiece, the 1972 Countach, a wedge-shaped V12 wonder that was plastered across every

The Gallardo (left, in Italian police guise) is the most affordable of Lamborghini's cars today, but the marque made its name with beautiful cars such as the Miura (below) and dramatic ones such as the Countach (opposite).

schoolboy's bedroom wall in the 1970s. Other noteworthy Lamborghinis included the four-seater Espada and the smaller Urraco/Jalpa series.

Ferruccio Lamborghini sold out of his sports car division in 1971, and died in 1993. After several changes of ownership, the marque was finally acquired by Audi i 1998. By that time, the 200 mph Diablo had replaced the Countach, and since then Audi has bankrolled the launch of a new supercar, the Murcielago, and a new 'junior' Lamborghini, the V10 Gallardo.

Happily, the low-slung bonnets of all these cars have sported the fighting bull emblem, still in a black shield. The only variation along the way has been the Lamborghini LM, an extraordinary 4x4 off-roader of the late 1980s, which carried the 'Lamborghini' corporate script, with its unusually curvaceous and looped capito 'L' as a decal along its bluff body sides. Yet even that had the traditional black badge on its towering bonnet.

LANCHESTER

In 1895, on a gloomy December day in Birmingham, Britain's first contribution to motoring fired into life. Twenty-seven-year-old engineer Frederick Lanchester eased his 'motorized carriage' forward over its first historic yards. However, unlike other pioneer car makers, Lanchester designed the whole thing from scratch, including the centrally located single-cylinder engine, with not one component from a horsedrawn vehicle or steam engine. It had a silent two-speed gearbox, was steered by a tiller and featured spring suspension and a stiff, tubular chassis giving – for the time – an astoundingly comfortable ride. It could also do an illegal 15 mph on flat roads (cars, preceded by red flag-bearers, were governed at 4 mph).

Two years later he completed a new, more powerful Lanchester, with a superb 3.5-litre twin-cylinder engine, and in 1899 the Lanchester Engine Company put it into production. The idiosyncrasies of the Lanchester, like its bonnet-less nose – the

engine was mid-mounted – and lack of a steering wheel often obscured its merits to buyers. Yet it was probably the quietest and most advanced car available anywhere.

By the time the 38 hp was launched in 1911, its six-cylinder engine was smoother still, while Lanchester had even caved in and offered an optional steering wheel. After the First World War, Lanchester came up with the 40 hp to rival the Rolls-Royce Silver Ghost. It now had a conventional bonnet and radiator grille shell. Still, where most cars had a radiator badge, the Lanchester had an in-built water level gauge; just below this, a modest and totally unembellished rectangular nameplate was adopted, with 'LANCHESTER' spelt out in silver letters on a black background.

Fine cars as Lanchesters were, the firm was battered by the aftermath of the 1929 Wall Street crash. It was taken over by Daimler in 1931, and Lanchesters were rapidly assimilated into the Daimler range. Simultaneously, the Lanchester badge was

given more flourish; the top edge gained a pitch to match the profile of the radiator shell, and 'LANCHESTER' was expressed in letters that ebbed and flowed in size, peaking between the 'H' and 'E', while the horizontal stroke of the 'L' was elongated to underline the entire word. Frederick Lanchester died in 1946 after having taken out over four hundred patents, which included disc brakes, the turbocharger and power steering. Lanchester cars lasted only another ten years. Post-war Lanchesters had a revised badge, now triangulated downwards and creased in the centre to suit a more pointed prow. The biggest version stretched almost across the whole radiator of the 1954 Lanchester Sprite, tapering to an end with the aid of ten vertical black enamel stripes either side of the name, but only prototypes were made before Daimler ditched the venerable name in 1956.

LANCIA

Lancia's is truly an aristocrat among car badges. Vincenzo Lancia, who began making his excellent luxury motor cars in 1908, employed his friend Count Carlo Biscaretti di Ruffia – later to become Italy's leading motoring historian – to design him a badge for them. What he came up with was a dark-blue flag bearing the Lancia name, the horizontal stroke of the large, flourishing 'L' underlining the 'A' and half of the 'N', and the whole hung to the left on a lance as a witty play on his friend's name. This emblem was superimposed over the circular outline of a four-spoke steering wheel infilled with white and featuring, on the horizontal right-hand spoke, the simple detail of the hand throttle that was then customary on the steering wheel of cars.

At some point not long afterwards, the whole badge was framed in a contrasting dark-blue shield; in 1957, with the advent of the high-tech Lancia Flaminia– a car with up-to-the-minute body design by Pininfarina – the entire steering wheel element was dispensed with. The Lancia

badge then became a raised chrome outline device, almost doubled in overall size, fixed to the mesh of the radiator grille rather than incorporated into its surrounding chromework. There was a shield-shaped perimeter line and an inner circle, while the lance carried the rectangular flag with the 'LANCIA' word on it much as before, but chrome on dark blue.

When Lancia launched the Delta in 1979, however, the badge made a sudden return to its noble roots. It was now a flat design once more, the four-spoke steering wheel was back, and the blue-and-white colour scheme was as it had been before the First World War, although the 'LANCIA' word was now in evenly uniform capitals without the languid 'L'. Only that old-fashioned hand throttle had been consigned to history.

LAND ROVER

A Land Rover is a versatile, no-nonsense vehicle, originally Britain's 4x4 answer to the US Jeep and today a leading worldwide brand of sport-utility vehicle (SUV). The badge has been similarly iconic from the start: the first models, of 1948, carried an oval aluminium casting, like a capsule pill in profile, attached to their wire mesh grilles. Raised bare aluminium letters on a black-painted background put 'LAND' in the upper-left part of the shape and 'ROVER' in the lower-right, and they were linked by what Land Rover calls 'the hyphens', a z-shaped squiggle. It was there to leave onlookers in no doubt that the two words were separate. A back-plate in a similar format sometimes added the words 'SOLIHULL, WARWICKSHIRE' and 'ENGLAND' in the spare space.

The badge remained on all Land Rovers until the Series III of 1971, whereupon it was changed to a narrow rectangle with 'LAND-ROVER' on it as part of a new grille design. Curiously, Land Rover the brand name was never hyphenated,

even though the badge was; this anomaly ended in 1984 when nameplates gained the more specific 'LAND ROVER 90' and 'LAND ROVER 110' legends.

In 1989 Land Rover diversified into the burgeoning SUV market with its Discovery. It was the first with a new Land Rover badge, a lustrously green ellipse with 'LAND ROVER' and the distinctive squiggle/hyphen in gold. Smaller than before, it sat on a raised plinth in the centre of the Discovery's plastic grille. This badge rapidly became standard across the Land Rover range, including the Freelander, but moved to a new position in the bottom-right quarter of the grille, where it has remained.

The 1970 Range Rover was a radical departure for Land Rover, mixing for the first time its traditional go-anywhere capability with something approaching luxury and style. Instead of a badge, 'R-A-N-G-E R-O-V-E-R' was spelt out in decals on the leading edge of the bonnet, and not until 1990 did Land Rover's badge appear in its new home in the right-hand corner of the grille.

LEXUS

The 1989 Lexus LS400, Toyota's all-new rival to the best large luxury saloons from Europe and the USA, was perhaps a surprisingly bland-looking car. The first Lexus model of all, it certainly did not stand out beside slinky Jaguars, star-spangled Cadillacs and coolly Teutonic Mercedes-Benzes. Its logo was similarly bland, little more than an 'L' in an ellipse, and decidedly plain besides Jaguar's famous 'big cat' and Mercedes' three-pointed star. It has not changed at all since. Why not? Let the US version of the Lexus Guidelines booklet explain:

"The symbol mark consists of a stylized Lexus 'L' connected to an open-ended ellipse that signifies the company's ever-expanding technological advancement and the limitless opportunities which lie ahead. The Lexus symbol mark cannot be disassembled; the 'L' and the ellipse must always be used together. The logotype (text version of 'LEXUS') is represented by specially created letterforms that spell the Lexus name. These two registered trademarks form the most significant feature of Lexus products and corporate identity and must never be altered."

Emotional it's not, but then Toyota always intended Lexus cars to be judged for what they are, not what they stand for. And subsequently the LS400 followed by the LS430, GS300, SC430, IS200 and RX300 models have scored consistently near-perfect results in customer satisfaction surveys (for example, the influential J.D. Power survey) in both the USA – the key market for Lexus – and Europe. An utterly straightforward badge is all that's been needed.

US Lexus owners, however, may be amazed to hear that the brand has not until now been sold in Japan. That is shortly to change, as Lexus is scheduled for its Japanese debut in 2005. The company is breaking totally new ground in product terms too: it is the first manufacturer anywhere to market a petrol-electric hybrid sport utility vehicle.

LINCOLN

The Lincoln marque, founded in 1920 and named after President Abraham Lincoln, has been used by American presidents since 1923. President John F. Kennedy, for example, was travelling in his stretched Lincoln Continental when he was assassinated in 1963. Ever since Henry Ford bought the company in 1922 and put his son Edsel in charge, Lincoln had a reputation for innovation and large, imposing cars. The 1937 Lincoln Zephyr was America's first successful aerodynamic production car. Edsel Ford said, "Father made the most popular car in the world. I would like to make the best". He was referring to the beautiful Lincoln Continental of 1940.

Lincoln's first car emblem was a florid brass affair, its overall shape looking not unlike a clown's heavily made-up mouth with corners turned down, laurel garlands on the 'lips', a small pagoda roof on top and the bottom tip of a shield visible at the bottom. 'LINCOLN' was prominent in serifed black enamel letters. In 1925 this was replaced by a simple black oval with white letters, and by 1932 this had morphed into a horizontally elongated ellipse enfolding the word 'LINCOLN'. It sat on a brass plaque, the stepped levels of which were gathered together in a stubby stem at top and bottom, the infill colour a dark-blue cloisonné enamel. In 1935 Lincoln's badge stayed blue but turned circular and featured 'LINCOLN' and 'V12' in Art Deco typography; the Zephyr was given a teardrop-shaped blue enamel logo with 'LINCOLN ZEPHYR V12' on it. Both were fixed to the cars' radiator grilles.

Then, suddenly, a heraldic crest appeared. A promotional film at the time said, "Symbolizing a high degree of quality and good taste is the new crest that decorates the prow of all 1942 Lincoln cars". There has been vague speculation that it was derived from the Lincoln family's crest, but it was almost certainly a Ford-instigated design in response to the crest on contemporary Cadillacs, which were then out-selling their Lincoln rivals. It was shield-shaped with a green cross splitting the central area into four. A gold star sat in the centre, and diagonally opposite were dotted, louvred quarters, finished in white, while the crowning image was the bust of a knight gazing through a slit in his helmet. Proof that this was far from any genuine Lincoln clan crest came after the Second World War, when Lincoln redesigned and widened it, perhaps after complaints from Packard, which featured a similar knight on its emblem. The cross was now red; the bottom left and top right louvred fields were now blue; and the knight had now turned to face head-on, staring through four eye-slits. It was utterly ersatz heritage.

Despite deploying the crest in various settings, the star element proved most lasting. Recast with four points and given a quartic frame, this 'continental star' chimed in conveniently with the Continental name that was revived in 1956, and made a fitting riposte to Mercedes-Benz's three-pointed star. This emblem has survived in dozens of designs (including as free-standing ornaments) through to today's models.

Opposite: the sumptuous 2003 Lincoln Navicross concept car showcases on its bodywork, and even incorporates into the backs of the seats, the marque's four-pointed star emblem, which is itself a remnant from an ersatz heraldic crest introduced in 1942.

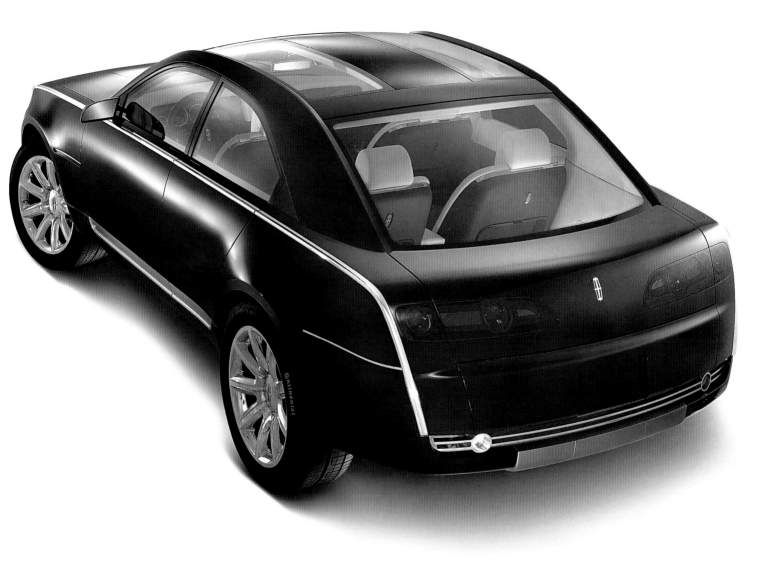

LOTUS

The Lotus badge design is based on that of a camshaft lobe, suiting the sportily hardcore nature of the cockpits of early cars (right); it is also shown here on the best-selling Elise (opposite), and the wing of the Vauxhall Lotus-Carlton (bottom).

When Anthony Colin Bruce Chapman founded Lotus in 1947, it was to soup up Austin Sevens in a shed behind a north London pub. But his irrepressible genius meant that he was soon building outstanding sports and racing cars. (He chose the name Lotus after the legendary plant, whose fruit is said to induce a state of forgetful bliss; that is, once you've driven a Lotus, you'll forget all other sports cars!)

Chapman was smart enough to employ an army of talented engineers and designers to make it all happen but, with the formation of Lotus Cars Ltd in 1955, every model carried his own four initials cleverly melded into a monogram above the fanned-out 'LOTUS' word in yellow; in fact the monogram dwarfed the 'LOTUS' letters. Both were set within an approximately triangular shape (pointing upwards) like the lobe of a camshaft, neatly fashioned by one of Chapman's junior draughtsmen, coloured a verdant green after the British Racing colour and placed on a bright yellow circular plaque.

The green-and-yellow livery featured on all Lotus racing cars until sponsorship – and tobacco advertisements – took over. A black-and-chrome version of the badge first appeared on an Elan sports car built for Lotus sales director Graham Arnold in 1967 as a special one-off car. A year later black badges were placed on all new cars made for a month after the death of double world champion Jim Clark in his Lotus Type 48 in a German Formula 2 race in April 1968. One or two further cars have been seen with black badges, but Lotus chroniclers have found no significance in this, apart from the batch of one hundred Esprits made in 1978 that featured them to commemorate Lotus winning the world championship for the seventh time.

In 1983, however, with Chapman dead and new shareholders in control, the unthinkable happened – this internationally recognized badge was ditched in favour of an uninspiring replacement. Fat, silver, overlapping 'LOTUS' letters spelt out the marque's name and were cocooned in

NAN 600D

Badge redesign (opposite, second from left) caused uproar among Lotus aficionados, even though Lotus sports cars have varied enormously over the years from the wedge-shaped Excel (opposite, below) to the Seven (below) and Elan (left).

a kind of flattened teardrop shape with a point at its peak, but there was no sign of the famous initials. First fitted to the Esprit Turbo, it looked more like the label in a cheap suit than the moniker of one of Britain's top sports cars.

It is thought that Lotus was, at the time, trying to distance itself from close association with Colin Chapman, after he was heavily implicated in the scandal of DeLorean's missing millions (Lotus had engineered the DeLorean DMC-12 for the US entrepreneur). Yet the outcry from Lotus owners and supporters – long before the days when campaigns could gather pace on the internet, of course – was such that, within months, the ACBC monogram was reinstated, albeit rendered very small. General Motors bought Lotus in 1987 and two years later the old badge was back for good, apart from another outing for the black badge on a limited edition 'Heritage' Lotus Elise. All in all, it was an object lesson in tampering with heritage at your peril, particularly one as venerated as Lotus's.

NMB 852H

175

MASERATI

Maserati is so marinated in its own heritage, one might assume its roots stretched back to the dawn of motoring time, rather than 'just' to 1926. Still, it does have a history longer than Porsche's – and even than that of Ferrari, which is Maserati's guardian now. Founded in 1926 by the four competition-mad Maserati brothers, the Italian company built only racing cars for its first twenty years; by 1934 it was the world's largest manufacturer of single-seaters.

Maserati's distinctive trademark, created in 1926 at the same time as its first two-seater car, the Tipo 26, was inspired by the Fountain of Neptune in Bologna's Piazza del Nettuno, which features a bronze sculpture of Neptune brandishing a three-pronged trident to hold back the sea. Initially this was an up-ended rectangle in polished brass with 'MASERATI' across the bottom, its letters almost touching the unframed edges of the badge, while above it an intricate rendering of the three-pointed trident's

head was engraved. In 1933 the badge was redesigned to incorporate Bologna's traditional blue-and-red insignia. A lemon-like vertical oval was the new outline; the lower quarter was in dark-blue with 'MASERATI' in silver, and the rest was white with the trident prongs in red. Around the edge ran a dark-blue keyline.

The company launched a road car only after the Second World War when the founders had gone and new owners, the Orsi family, decided to capitalize on the marque's track-honed reputation. It was easier said than done. Maserati's racing success was based on precision engineering and painstaking testing, and these disciplines transferred slowly to the showroom. By 1955, after nine years of production, only 139 road cars had been sold, and there was only one dealer – in Rome.

The badge naturally transferred to the new A6G2000 road car, their extremely sporty bodies provided by outside coachbuilders. One of these, Carrozzeria

Zagato of Milan, festooned the grille of one coupé with a stark modern interpretation of the trident – similar to a three-pronged TV aerial – in 1955, and from then on almost every Maserati had both an enamel badge and a chrome cut-out of the trident, generally reverting to a more historically authentic rendition on its radiator grille. On bespoke-bodied cars, this was usually the centrepiece of a fancy chrome frame, which sometimes put the trident in a circle, but the design protocol of a bonnet badge and a grille trident survives to this day.

Despite a shave with bankruptcy in 1958, the Orsis turned Maserati into a luxury brand with the 3500GT, a powerful and beautiful car boasting plenty of engineering parallels with the race-winning 350S and 250F. It caused a splash at its public debut in Geneva in 1957. Sales took off when the US market opened in 1961. Maserati gradually moved away from race cars altogether, and throughout the 1960s served up a bewildering array

of models that made enthusiasts' mouths water.

Maserati's life as a corporate entity, however, lurched from crisis to crisis: as the beautiful mid-engined Bora was sending the car media into ecstasy in 1971, the firm was in Citroën's possession, but the sales decimation caused by the mid-1970s oil crisis brought in the receivers in 1975. Fiery Argentinian supercar maker Alessandro de Tomaso came to the rescue. He reputedly paid just 210,000 lire – about £150 – for Maserati. A bargain … but it did come with £3.5 million of debt.

De Tomaso's vision for the marque led to a confrontation with BMW. In 1981 Maserati unveiled the first Biturbo, a 3 series rival with understated styling and plenty of performance. It also sported an encircled chrome trident motif on its C-pillars and what soon became a new trademark: an oval clock in the middle of the dashboard. For a while it sold well, but Maserati still did not have the capital to develop all-new cars. Fiat's 1993 buy-in and, five years

later, complete takeover didn't come a moment too soon.

In 1998 the wraps came off the 3200GT, the first modern-generation Maserati, and when it went on sale in 2000 it carried a subtly remodelled version of the venerable trident badge. The fine detail of the trident was tidied up to give it more impact, a less weighty black keyline replaced the blue one, and the delicately pointed ends of the oval were rounded off to create a perfect ellipse.

One weird aside to the Maserati story was the 1988 Chrysler TC by Maserati, a two-seater luxury convertible designed in Detroit but, for added cachet, built in Italy. Its radiator grille sported the bizarre compound logo of Chrysler's five-sided 'Pentastar' framing a Maserati trident.

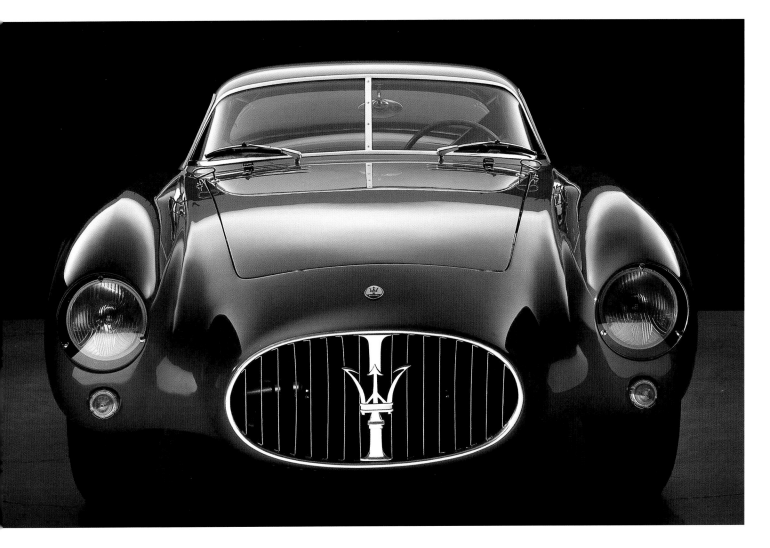

MAYBACH

Maybach's V12-engined cars were among the largest and costliest of the 1920s and 1930s; their spirit, prestige and, indeed, badge were revived in 2002 by Mercedes-Benz to create one of the most exclusive luxury saloons in the world.

The revived Maybach, the result of a long-held desire by Mercedes-Benz to put the marque back on the roads, is arguably the most convincing attempt yet to produce the ultimate in luxury saloons. Powered by a 500 bhp twin-turbocharged V12 engine, it went on sale in 2002 in two wheelbase versions, the Maybach 57 and 62. Interestingly, to underline their stately nature, the cars come not with a bonnet or grille badge but a mascot, also called a 'hood ornament' in the USA. A slightly modernized version of that seen on the original Maybach cars built between 1921 and 1941, it's an arrowhead, its three sides all curved, framing two intertwined 'M's, which once stood for 'Maybach Motorenbau' but are now short for 'Maybach Manufaktur'. Usually finished in gold on the pre-war cars, the new Maybach's mascot is in gleaming chrome. When seen on printed materials, however, the new logo also has a gold infill colour. Either way, it's nothing like as ostentatious as Rolls-Royce or Bentley insignia.

Willhelm Maybach partnered Gottlieb Daimler in designing the very earliest cars of all, but the two split in 1907. With his son Karl, Maybach then started producing engines for Count Zeppelin's airships. A magnificent V12 car engine was a natural progression from aircraft power units, but when no car maker would agree to fit it in their products, Maybach designed his own. Just two thousand of his cars were sold. They were phenomenally expensive, beautifully finished and near-silent; along with their mascot, they also had a radiator badge to match, bordered in white and with gold 'M's against red and later blue backgrounds. The Maybach Zeppelin of 1933–37 was perhaps the ultimate version. One of the largest cars of all time, its bonnet was seven feet long and the radiator three feet wide; a Ford Fiesta could fit inside its twelve-foot wheelbase.

After the Second World War, Maybach made diesel railway locomotive engines until 1960, when the company was finally acquired by Daimler-Benz.

MAZDA

The original Mazda logo (left) was often seen on a triangular plinth, as on this 1971 RX-3 coupé (below), to hint at the rotary engine inside; bottom: the 1991–97 logo, seen here on a Mazda Xedos 6; opposite: the second-generation Mazda MX-5 with the company's 'spreading fan' badge.

The first Mazda car in 1959 bore the simple signature of a stylized 'm' in a circle, the left-hand stem of the letter extending upwards to meet the roof of the circle and the right-hand one dropping down to join the circle's floor. In the 1970s this logo was often seen framed in a three-sided shape representing a cross-section of the combustion chamber in the rotary engines fitted to such Mazdas as the RX-2 and RX-3. Some other models, such as the 929 and 818, carried the 'm' on a fancy triangular plinth attached to the top of the radiator grille, while cars made in the years 1975–91, such as the RX-7, carried merely the 'MAZDA' word in a high-tech-style typeface nameplate that mixed lower-case 'a's with capitals and a 'Z' expressed as if drawn through a stencil.

In 1991 Mazda launched an all-new badge – an oval chrome ring with a blob on a stalk inside: "the characteristics of wings, sun and circle of light" was the official explanation of the vague symbolism. The Japanese manufacturer was clearly struggling to find the right badge design, because only six years later it introduced its now-familiar current logo, which made its debut on the Mazda 626 as a heavy chrome outline. The work of corporate identity creative expert called Rei Yoshimara, it was instigated after Ford upped its shareholding in Mazda to 33.4%.

According to Mazda: "the 'V' in the centre of the 'M' spreads out like an opening fan, representing the creativity, the sense of mission, the gentleness and flexibility, the resoluteness and vitality that are Mazda. Poised like wings ready to fly, the 'V' is also a starting point for future growth. The symbol as a whole represents the sharp, solid feeling that Mazda will be seeking in all its products. The dynamic circle symbolizes Mazda ready to spread its wings as it enters the twenty-first century."

Still, it looked remarkably similar to the trademark of a chain of garages in the east of England called Mann Egerton. No such fancy explanation for that: it simply represented a tern on the wing.

MERCEDES-BENZ

The invention of the automobile in the 1880s inspired Gottlieb Daimler and Karl Benz, independently of one another, to become pioneers in this new form of transport. With the help of financial backers, they both launched their projects privately in Mannheim, Germany. Benz founded Benz & Cie in October 1883, while Daimler-Motoren-Gesellschaft (DMG) was formed in November 1890. Both companies used the names of their founders in text as trademarks, instead of symbols or made-up trade names along 'Acme' lines. Benz adopted a cog wheel symbol in 1903, replacing it with a laurel wreath surrounding the name 'BENZ' in 1909. By the turn of the century, however, DMG had launched a completely new trade name for its products: Mercedes.

Mercedes (Spanish for 'grace') was the name of the daughter born to Austrian businessman Emil Jellinek in 1889. In 1897 he visited Daimler at its new factory in Cannstatt to order a car, and the following year he ordered two faster Daimler

Phoenix examples – the world's first four-cylinder cars. Jellinek was soon promoting and selling DMG's wares to his wealthy friends and contacts. By 1900 he had ordered over forty vehicles, and had driven Daimlers at race meetings such as the Nice week event, where he raced under his nickname, 'Monsieur Mercédès'. He was such an influential character for Daimler that in April 1900 the firm agreed to let him sell the cars under the Mercedes name. Sales snowballed to such an extent that by September 1902 Mercedes had been registered as the trade name for all Daimler's cars. A year later and Jellinek had even renamed himself officially as Emil Jellinek-Mercedes, commenting wryly that it was "probably the first time that a father has taken his daughter's name".

Despite this, DMG still lacked a characteristic trademark. Then Paul and Adolf Daimler – the company founder's two sons, who were now in charge of the business – remembered that their father had once used a star as a symbol when

Right: the logical merger of the Mercedes and Benz badges to create the world-famous logo of today; below: the C111 concept car of 1970 impressed with its 'gullwing' doors, and also its bold use of the Mercedes-Benz logo.

employed as technical director of the Deutz gas engine factory from 1872 until 1881. Once he had marked a star above his own house on a picture postcard of Cologne and Deutz, and wrote to his wife that this star would one day shine over his own factory to symbolize prosperity. In June 1909 both three- and four-pointed stars were registered as trademarks, although only the three-pointed star was ever used. It was supposed to symbolize Daimler's tripartite ambition of motorized power on land, water and in the air.

From 1910 it began to appear as a design feature on the cars' radiator grille surround, either in the centre at the top or, when the cars featured a V-shaped radiator shell from 1912, on both profiles. But changes soon followed. In 1916 the points were surrounded by a circle, in which four small stars and the word 'Mercedes', or sometimes the names of the DMG plants at Untertürkheim or Berlin-Marienfelde, were incorporated. During this period, a three-dimensional star, in a

Left: the star/roundel in a bold new iteration, slightly embedded in the nose of the 208 mph Mercedes-Benz SLR McLaren; below, left: the badges on today's cars show remarkable consistency since the 1930s days of cars such as the 540K (below, right).

circle, became a graphically striking radiator cap mascot, which remains largely unchanged in form on Mercedes-Benz saloon cars today. In November 1921 DMG applied for patents for any new variations on its easily recognized trademark, and it was registered in August 1923.

Daimler and Benz, the two oldest motor manufacturers on the planet, merged in June 1926, forming Daimler-Benz AG. The company's products were renamed Mercedes-Benz. The three-pointed star mascot continued, but the badge united the Mercedes star with the Benz laurels. The star was in white-enamelled relief on a domed, heavily textured silver background, while a sober dark-blue outer ring carried 'MERCEDES' at the top and 'BENZ' below, separated by two sprigs of laurel leaves. A third version of the trademark is a large chrome star in relief, first seen as part of the radiator grille design on the beautiful 300SL 'Gullwing' sports car in 1952.

Apart from almost indiscernible fettling,

these three-star versions have hardly changed since. What has been altered, however, is the combination in which they are presented. The C Class in 1986 signalled the end of the practice of both mascot and badge appearing on traditional Mercedes-Benz saloons: they now come just with the mascot. Sporty models have the badge and the radiator decoration but no mascot, while smaller, family cars such as the A Class tend to come with just the decoration.

MERCURY

Just as when it was launched in 1939, Mercury is a brand positioned in the market midway between Ford and Lincoln, and since that very beginning it has generally had more of a perfomance accent than its stablemates.

Mercury was the creation of Edsel Ford, son of Henry, who considered 103 different names for it before eventually settling on Ford-Mercury. Ford designers dutifully created a badge using the familiar Ford oval sitting atop 'MERCURY' in block capitals, but then Ford had a change of mind and the car was unveiled in October 1939 as the Mercury 8, a completely separate marque. It didn't have a badge as such; instead the word 'MERCURY' and the figure '8' was incorporated into its impressive chrome grille.

At the 1939–40 New York world's fair, Ford displayed the cars alongside a twenty-five-foot statue in stainless steel of Mercury, the Roman god of trade and travel, complete with a winged helmet for added fleetness; the Greeks knew him as Hermes. The image was used in brochures, too, but it didn't appear as a badge on a Mercury car until the stylish 1949 range was unveiled, where it comprised the upper element in a faux-historic coat of arms grille badge. Over the years Mercury gradually turned to face the right in profile, but between 1960 and 1985 the coat of arms was mostly phased out in favour of individual model liveries, such as that on the 1967 Mercury Cougar, which included a prowling big cat emblem on its radiator grille.

In the 1970s an upstanding and brittle-looking chrome bonnet ornament began to be fitted to such cars as the Mercury Monarch, featuring an 'M' in a circle, and this gave rise to a new circular Mercury emblem in 1985: three parallel kinked lines in chrome across a black, chrome-edged circle detailed the three stems of the previous capital 'M'. Emboldened by thicker chrome lines, this is what we see on the grilles of Mercurys today.

MG

The MGF (opposite) of 1995 encapsulated everything Cecil Kimber's Morris Garages strove for in small, affordable and fun sports cars; this page, top to bottom: the MG TD; the octagonal badge on a recent MG saloon; the badge on an MGB and highlighted by the bonnet moulding.

First, there is a myth to dispel about the MG badge: its octagonal shape was not created because of an octagonal dining table belonging to company founder Cecil Kimber; nor after the eight-sided prison building in MG's home town of Abingdon-on-Thames, Oxfordshire, UK. The MG logo was, in fact, drawn up by an MG accountant called Edmund Lee in 1923, who was a keen amateur artist, and he was influenced by the contemporary Art Deco movement. When Kimber saw Lee's sketches, he declared: "That's just the thing." It appeared on advertisements in 1923, was registered as a trademark in 1924, and made it to the radiator grille of the Morris-based MG 14/40 MkIV in 1928.

Possibly influenced by the livery of the local Great Western Railway, Kimber opted for chocolate brown 'MG' initials (they stood for the firm's origins as Morris Garages) and octagonal frame, all edged in chrome, on a cream background. This colour scheme gave rise to racing MGs being painted brown and cream, and so

being nicknamed 'cream crackers'.

The badge remained unchanged until the demise of the MGA in 1962. With the launch of the MGB that year, the badge changed to silver letters and surround on a red background. It was now mounted on a black shield and was actually incorporated into the car's styling – the slightly raised position of the badge on the car's prow led to a distinctive tapering ridge on the MGB's bonnet. In 1975 the badge colours changed to gold on red to celebrate MG's official fiftieth birthday, changed to silver on black a year after, and to black on red for the launch of the Metro in 1982.

MG returned to two-seater sports cars in 1992 with the RV8, simultaneously reviving the brown-and-cream badge. This has since been worn by a large array of new models, especially after a change of ownership in 2000 when BMW's six-year custodianship of MG ended and the brand was reinvigorated. As Britain's most popular sporting marque, MG is expected to survive MG Rover's recent insolvency.

MINI

Right, top: until 1969, Minis wore individual marque identities, such as Austin; right, centre: from 1997 to 2000, this was the Mini's nostalgic badge style; right, bottom: the bolder, relaunched Mini logo; opposite: the Mini Cooper cabriolet.

'Mini' became a marque in its own right in 1969, ten years after the revolutionary front-wheel drive, transverse-engined economy car was launched by the British Motor Corporation. Before then it was sold as an Austin, a Morris, a Riley and a Wolseley, but it was already referred to universally as simply the Mini, hence the change.

The car's shape, the work of Sir Alec Issigonis, was its trademark, so minimal emphasis was placed on giving it a distinctive badge. A small black plastic shield carried 'MINI' at the top in silver above an extremely basic silver arrowhead shape divided in two by a black line. This lasted until 1978, when it was replaced by an identically sized shield in blue with only the British Leyland corporate symbol, but the old style returned in 1980 and remained for eleven further years. From 1991 the shield's contents were changed: this time 'MINI' was spelt out in silver-edged red letters on a black background with a red dividing line.

With the original Mini's final revamp in 1997, the badge adopted a nostalgic design that, ironically, had never been seen on any Mini before. Four heavily chromed horizontal bars, narrowing in width from top to bottom, stuck out from either side of a thickly chromed circle framing a domed plastic medallion. This 'MINI' was in silver inside a silver ring on a dark-green background.

Between 1994 and 2000 BMW owned the remains of British Leyland; despite selling Rover and MG to its management and Land Rover to Ford, it retained Mini and relaunched the brand in spectacular fashion; the all-new Mini has been voted North American Car of the Year and in 2004 production reached half a million. Its badge is a natural progression of that fitted to 1997–2000 Minis, now using black and silver but with the four bars smoothed into triangular wings either side of a much enlarged circle with a thinner chrome ring. It's a pleasing design that manages to revisit the sporty if well-worn 'wing' theme without appearing old-fashioned.

MITSUBISHI

Mitsubishi's triple-diamond logo has been on every car the company has built, even this attractive Colt cabriolet from the early 1960s shown below; opposite: the badge he recently joined the here and abandoned its traditional red colour for straightforward chrome finish.

The Mitsubishi logo is an interesting example of the multi-layered symbolism underpinning many Japanese trademarks.

Yataro Iwasaki founded Tsukumo Shokai as a shipping line in 1870. Japan was emerging from centuries of feudal isolation and Iwasaki's ambitious business plans reflected the country's race to catch up with the West as a trading nation. He hailed from the city of Kochi on the island of Shikoku, which was home to the powerful Tosa clan for whom he had once worked and from whom he leased his first three steam ships. The three-diamond mark – the genesis of the Mitsubishi logo – put in an early appearance on one vessel, chosen by Iwasaki as it signified both the three oak leaves of his Tosa mentors' crest and also the three stacked diamonds of his own family crest. Conveniently, it also represented the three blades of a ship propeller. In 1874 the shipping company was renamed Mitsubishi Shokai, and a Japanese government grateful for his

buccaneering enterprise rewarded Iwasaki with favourable contracts. The company eventually became a cornerstone of today's NYK line.

The name Mitsubishi is a combination of the Japanese words *mitsu* and *hishi*. *Mitsu* means 'three' and *hishi* actually means 'water chestnut', although the Japanese have long used the word as a metaphor for a rhombus or diamond shape. Japanese often bend the 'h' sound to a 'b' sound when it occurs in the middle of a word. So they pronounce the combination of *mitsu* and *hishi* as 'mitsubishi'.

Diversification followed later under the aegis of Iwasaki's son Hisaya – everything from coal and copper mining to shipbuilding, property, banking, paper mills and even backing the Kirin Brewery. In 1917 Mitsubishi announced the Model A, Japan's very first private car. Only twenty of them were built before the venture was abandoned. After the Second World War the Allied occupation forces insisted the

This progression (left) demonstrates how diamonds, oak leaves and ship's propellers have influenced the Mitsubishi badge, which is shown on this page in various positions on recent production and concept cars.

Mitsubishi empire disband into 139 separate companies, and most ditched the three-diamond logo. Mitsubishi Heavy Industries was one that didn't.

What led to Mitsubishi Heavy Industries becoming a player in the motor industry was its Silver Pigeon scooter and Mizushima three-wheeled pick-up, both introduced in 1946; in 1960 it launched a rear-engined 500 cc economy car, a vehicle rather like Italy's Fiat 500, which sported Mitsubishi's red three-diamond logo as a badge. This logo has been an absolute constant on every Mitsubishi since 1960, except in the early export days when they were sold under the Dodge name in the USA, and in 1975 when they were exported to the UK and sold as Colt cars. Even these guises, presumably adopted because Mitsubishi was worried about Western acceptance of its Oriental-sounding title, were soon dropped.

By 1970 the company offered a full car range for everyone, from city dwellers to tycoons. That was the year Mitsubishi

Motors became an independent company, while in 2003 it was reborn again as the new Mitsubishi Motors, a manufacturer specializing in passenger cars. Times have been hard for the company of late, with major investor DaimlerChrysler pulling out, but Mitsubishi is fighting back with new models such as the Grandis and Colt. These have a feature that began to appear on Mitsubishi's concept show cars in the latter half of the 1990s: a Mitsubishi logo embedded in the frontal design and – for the first time – coloured not red but a cool grey.

MORGAN

The Morgan shape, including the rounded nose cowling and winged badge (right, below) are copyright-protected. The idiosyncratic British marque was founded on three-wheelers (right), but its most famous model is the Plus 8 (opposite).

The latest Morgan, the flamboyantly designed and very fast Aero 8, is the first Morgan in a long time not to sport a badge on its rounded radiator cowling. A very long time, in fact, as the last one was probably from Morgan's pre-First World War days as a British maker of three-wheeler economy cars that just happened to be very competitive in motor sport events like cross-country trials. At that time, the motorcycle engines fitted to Morgans, which were introduced in 1909, stuck out of the front of the cars (the single wheel was at the rear). As they were air-cooled, there was no radiator, but from 1921 the Family model had a dummy one fitted anyway for decency's sake, with a brass surround carrying an interesting rendition of 'Morgan' as a script radiator badge, the left-hand serif of the 'M' turning into a coil and the ear and loop of the 'g' helping the flow of the letters look cohesive on the domed front of the car.

Morgan had a change of direction in 1936 when it launched its first four-wheeled car, the 4/4, which is the longest-running model name on any car ever – a version is still on sale in 2005 alongside the Aero 8. This is the car that has pretty much defined the classic profile of Morgans to this day – a shape that is now, uniquely in the car world, protected under copyright.

With the 4/4 came a new badge. At its centre was a circle with an inner section given a gravelly texture in contrast to a smooth outer band. Across this was a black cross, its longitudinal bar carrying the 'MORGAN' word while its vertical represented the '/' between the '4' and the '4'. Gently curved wings (more benign-looking, somehow, than the plumage on other sporting cars' badges) protruded from either side.

This badge, which since 1953 has transferred from a position on the front of the old flat radiator grille to a central spot above the grille on the curved nose cowling, endured on every Morgan up until the Aero 8's unveiling in 2000. It was, of course, modified for such models as

the Plus 4 and Plus 8, with a '+' character on the upper part of the vertical where necessary, and usually enamelled black on a chrome base. However, the early 'Morgan' script with its curly-tipped 'M' has also endured to this day as the corporate wordage style (if such an ugly term can be applied to the organization, which is still family-owned).

MORRIS

The first car designed by William Morris (not to be confused with his namesake, leader of Britain's Arts and Crafts movement) was often called the 'Bullnose' Morris, even though its real title was the Morris Oxford, after the English city where it was made. The nickname was a shortening of 'bullet nose', an earlier moniker given because the domed top of the radiator shell looked like a 0.303 bullet. But it was highly appropriate because an ox crossing a ford is intrinsic to the coat of arms of Oxford. This bovine image, in the form of a red animal striding across three wavy blue lines, was placed in a shield in the centre of the dark-blue radiator badge, with 'MORRIS' arrayed across the top and 'COWLEY' or 'OXFORD', both the names of Morris models, below.

By the 1930s the badge had become a shield itself; for the most famous Morris of all, the 1948 Minor, it sat in the centre of a chrome emblem not unlike the highly influential London Underground logo, a circle sitting at the midpoint of a chunky, ribbed bar. On the Series II, a chrome spire stuck up at the top and tapered to a point half-way towards the bonnet's peak.

Other Morris cars of the 1960s carried the shield under a round clear plastic dome, framed with a chrome ring. When the Minor was dropped in 1971, after over one and a half million had been sold, the Morris brand went into steady decline in parallel with the malaise of its parent company, British Leyland. There was no Morris badge at all on the front of the 1971 Marina, although later models carried the 'MORRIS' word annexed to the British Leyland symbol in a plastic strip. The Morris Ital of 1980 had the diagonally striped corporate band used to identify vehicles made by British Leyland's Austin-Morris division. The last Morris Ital was sold in 1984 when the marque name for cars was deemed so unappealing that it was abandoned altogether.

NISSAN

The chrome Nissan badge, which like those on rival marques has recently grown in size, is a circle crossed by a long rectangle, on which 'NISSAN' is written in black. Tidy but unremarkable, it looks a little like the much-emulated London Underground symbol.

When seen in colour as Nissan's corporate communications logo, however, it comes alive. Japan's national flag, used since 1870, salutes the country's motto of 'land of the rising sun': a red circle on a white background. Nissan adapted it with a blue bar across the middle of the sun to carry what it calls the 'Nissan Corporate Wordmark'. Further rationale for the colour scheme comes from the Japanese proverb 'Sincerity brings success'; according to Nissan, the red indicates sincerity and the blue the skies, meaning possibilities. However, the blue was changed to grey in 2001 when the trademark was spruced up by Renault, which had taken a controlling stake in the ailing company.

The Nissan Motor Company came into being on 26 December 1933. One of its

predecessor companies was DAT, financed by Messrs Den, Aoyama and Takeuchi, which had built Britain's Austin Seven under licence and called it the Datson (son of DAT); in 1933 this was changed to Datsun, as *son* in Japanese means 'loss'. The Datsun name remained Nissan's marketing tool for selling cars until 1 January 1984, when Nissan began the laborious process of unifying its corporate and trade names.

There wasn't really a Datsun badge to discard. The cars, which had successfully penetrated export markets such as the USA and the UK by the 1970s, had sufficed with the letter 'D' in silver on black or red, mounted in various shield-, oblong- and oval-shaped settings. Specialist models, such as the Z and Skyline performance cars, had individual liveries that cloaked their Datsun identity. In 1984 the 'NISSAN' mark was applied as a straightforward text nameplate to the cars' grilles, but in 1989 the badge we know today appeared, starting with the Maxima and Prairie, as each model was replaced or facelifted.

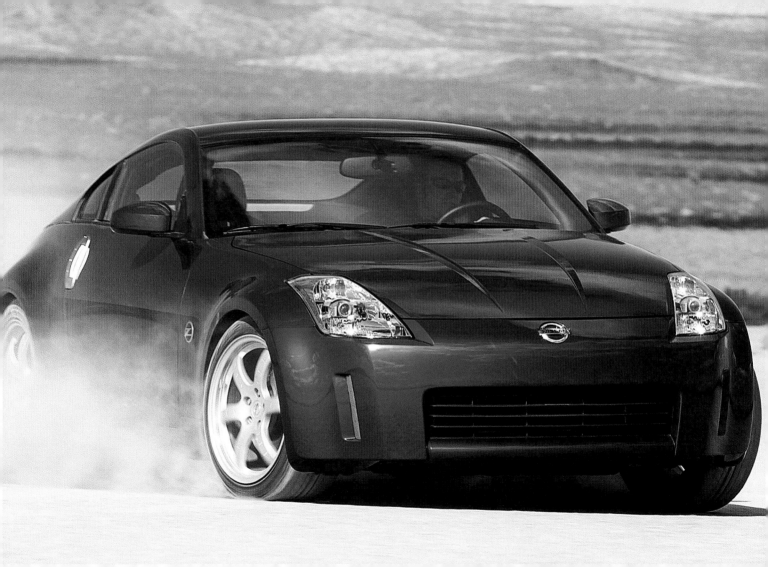

OLDSMOBILE

Oldsmobile's decorative crest (left) was among the first car badges ever, although it was initially fitted to the side of cars. It was replaced by an over-elaborate crest (far left), which endured until the GM brand switched to rocket imagery in 1949 (opposite).

Oldsmobile's announcement, in 1997, of a brand new logo to celebrate its centenary is one of the least prescient in motoring history. Within three years its owner, General Motors, gave it the chop, saying that the brand overlapped with other more successful ones in its portfolio. What was not said, but everyone knew, was that Oldsmobile had a dowdy image that had proved unshakeable.

So only Oldsmobiles built from 1997 until the very last car, a cherry red Alero, rolled down the production line in Lansing, Michigan, on 28 April 2004, bear an elliptical emblem showing a rocket taking off, its point jutting out of the chrome surround. It was a sad end to a motoring institution begun by Ransom Eli Olds in 1897, when he formed the Olds Motor Vehicle Company to capitalize on his design for a motorized carriage. He is credited with devising the first production line in 1901 to roll out the so-called 'curved dash' Oldsmobile.

Olds commissioned a crest especially for his new venture, and it was proudly carried on the cars' sides. A basic shield outline had feathered edges, a large red oval in the centre, a gold background and, across the centre line, a curly-ended scroll carrying 'OLDSMOBILE' diagonally from bottom right to top left. Hugging the oval at the top was 'OLDS MOTOR WORKS', with 'LANSING, MICH. U.S.A' around the base.

In 1908 Olds came under General Motors ownership, by which time the badge's colourway had changed to white oval and red background. GM eventually decided that Oldsmobile's crest was dated, and replaced it in 1929 with a similarly shield-shaped emblem consisting of a winged spur (to denote speed), three acorns (alluding to Mr Olds's mass-production intentions), oak leaves, the 'lamp of knowledge' and a micrometer and set-square (to portray the idea of precision). Coloured red, yellow and silver, it was placed in a black circle; at the bottom of a ribbed metal surround was

'OLDSMOBILE' with 'PRODUCT OF GENERAL MOTORS' written small beneath it.

GM's endeavour to shoehorn in so many motifs made the badge a bit bewildering; still, in various forms it adorned Oldsmobiles until 1948, when there was a complete change. Oldsmobile swapped 'heraldic' for 'space-age' by fitting a prominent new badge showing a gold-coloured globe, naturally centred on North and South America, surrounded by a chrome ring. It made its debut on Oldsmobile's first official pace car of the 1949 Indianapolis 500, the Rocket 88.

In 1959 Oldsmobile changed its logo again. Now the car carried the highly simplistic image of a rocket in vertical take-off, and variations of this continued until 1997. The 1994 Aurora was an ill-fated last try to revive consumer interest in Oldsmobile; it was a stylish saloon which, interestingly, carried no Oldsmobile identity at all. The end was signalled in December 2000, and the final tally was 35,229,218 Oldsmobiles in 107 years.

OPEL

Opel may have blurred the distinction between lightning and rockets in its logo development but the effect has been similar; opposite: everything significant the company has built in a proud display of formation parking.

Opel's chrome circle with a stylized fork of lightning streaking through it from left to right is familiar all over mainland Europe. It is General Motors' main European brand and, despite size changes, 'plasticization' on cars such as the 1982 Corsa, and being seen (as on the Manta) as a black skeletal decal, it is still broadly the same chrome emblem that first appeared on the 1962 Kadett.

German industrialist Adam Opel began in business in 1862 by making sewing machines, then bicycles, and in 1899 bought the nascent car business of Friedrich Lutzmann. One of his first acts was to stick a large cast nameplate on the front of the Lutzmann car. It was the Opel trademark, lemon-shaped in outline and with 'OPEL' in heavily serifed geometric letters – the 'O' resembling an upright diamond. The letters and outline were gold, the background black.

Until the First World War, Opels such as the 4/8 hp of 1909 (very popular with country doctors) came mostly with a large 'Opel' diagonal script in flat brass on the radiator mesh, the ascender of the 'p' curling round to join up with the tail of the loopy 'l' to underscore the marque's title. But in the 1920s and 1930s Opels reverted to the earlier style, now as a badge on the prow of the flat radiator shell, in dark-blue enamel on a brass base and with 'OPEL' in white letters.

Acquired by General Motors in 1929, Opel was extraordinarily successful: by 1935 it had claimed 42% of the German market, and it became the first German car maker with annual sales of one hundred thousand cars. In 1931 Opel introduced a new line of trucks called the Schnell-Lastwagen. It was soon rebranded to commemorate the company's foray into rocket-propulsion experiments in the 1920s, and Blitz (German for 'lightning') was chosen as the result of a naming competition in which Opel received one and a half million entries from the public. A new badge on its radiator grille reinforced the message: a circle with a finned, torpedo-like rocket set across it, heading right to left. Opel cars of the late 1930s also acquired a small torpedo bonnet ornament.

At the time, it seemed purely a symbol of speed and power. Ironically, however, the 3-ton Opel Blitz was to be the German army's main general purpose truck in the Second World War. Not surprisingly, when the Blitz truck resumed production in 1946 the emblem was absent, but it made a return on Opel's first all-new car, the 1953 Rekord. The circular outline and the rocket were in gold, the background black. Not until the Kadett in 1962 did the politically incorrect weaponry morph into the lightning streak.

PACKARD

The Packard badge is among the most elaborate and decorative ever to grace a production car. It's a golden coat of arms based around a cross of connected lozenges, with a rose distorted into quatrefoil in each red-enamelled quartering. On top of all this, nestling in an extravagant flourish of swirling branches surrounding a knight's armoured helmet, is a pelican 'in her piety' – that is, plucking at her own breast to feed her young.

The coat of arms belonged to the Packer family of Baddow, Essex, England, a dynasty with which James and Warren Packard, the founding brothers of the car firm, claimed strong links through their ancestor Samuel Packard, who migrated to America in the seventeenth century. They originally set out simply to improve the early Winton car that they had bought in 1899, and were soon in production with a much-developed 12 hp copy in Warren, Ohio. But less than two years later they had sold out to a Detroit businessman with the unlikely name of Henry B. Joy, who moved the whole shebang to Motown and rapidly turned Packard into one of the classic American marques of the 1920s and 1930s.

It was during this period that the badge appeared on the cars' yoke-shaped radiators, in an oval surround; until this time the most distinctive Packard features had been the radiator shape itself, and the hexagonal stampings on the cars' hubcaps, both of which were introduced in 1904.

In addition, pre-war Packards came with a plain radiator cap, which could be replaced by a choice of four factory-approved mascots. The first one featured a pair of wings under a Boyce motometer gauge; in 1924 you could have a Rolls-style flying lady; in 1927 sculptor Emil Bourdelle was commissioned to come up with an Adonis figure; and in 1931 the badge's pelican herself became three-dimensional (though people used to give it the nickname of 'the cormorant').

Packard took over Studebaker in 1954, and in 1958 the last Packard car (based on the Studebaker Hawk coupé) was made.

PANHARD-LEVASSOR

René Panhard and Emile Levassor were two Frenchmen with a lot of foresight. They established their partnership in 1889 and, after acquiring the exclusive rights in France to the patents for Daimler's internal combustion engine, they built their first car in 1890/91. Levassor's key breakthrough was in devising the template for the conventional car, which would predominate for the next seventy years: an engine mounted at the front under a bonnet and driving the rear wheels through clutch, gearbox and chains.

He even had a name for his novel concept: 'Système Panhard & Levassor'. And in what is almost certainly the first ever car to carry its own logo, an outsize roundel was painted on one car's vertical front panel covering the engine, the decoratively serifed monogram of a 'P' intertwined with an 'L' in a closely fitting circle. Thus bedecked, this car achieved the then incredible feat of driving from Paris to Nice in five days in 1893.

The 'PL' monogram was attached to the radiator grilles of the cars as Panhard-Levassor got into its stride as a car maker. In 1910 it introduced its first car with an engine featuring sleeves instead of conventional valves, and launched a new logo to herald this. The 'PL' and circle were simplified, the characters made less weighty and barely touching one another, while two 'S's were carried outside the circle's perimeter on little brackets. The double 'S' stood for *sans soupapes* – 'without valves'. By 1922 Panhard-Levassor only made sleeve-valve engines and the new badge became omnipresent. On the extravagantly styled Panhard Dynamic of 1937, it was carried as both an elaborate skeleton and a red-coloured 'solid' badge. (The manufacturer itself referred to its cars as Panhards from the start of the 1930s, rather cruelly casting aside Emile Levassor's name for the sake of snappiness.)

After the Second World War the logo was replaced by chrome decor on the Dyna economy models, and then a plain 'Panhard' script for the PL54 series that replaced it in 1953. However, a 'PL' circular motif, with the 'S's deleted, returned on the Panhard 24CT coupé in 1963, in red on a tan background within a chrome-bordered shield. Citroën took Panhard-Levassor over in 1965; car manufacture ended two years later.

PEGASO

The animal in the badge is Pegasus, the mythical flying horse from which the Pegaso name is derived. The white animal is seen flying across the centre of a black circle; the badge is mounted on a triangular plinth with the point facing downwards.

The debut of the Pegaso Z-102, an exclusive and sophisticated Spanish supercar, at the 1951 Paris motor show set the automotive world buzzing. It was designed by Spanish-born, ex-Alfa Romeo engineer Wilfredo Ricart. He was quite a character, dressing in Oriental-style jackets with sleeves that covered his hands, and wearing thick rubber-soled shoes that, he claimed, cushioned his brain.

Ricart had returned to his native Spain from Italy in 1946, where he joined the newly formed Empresa Nacional de Autocamiones SA (ENASA), a truck company formed by the government to meet a crippling nationwide shortage of vehicles. The trucks were sold under the Pegaso name, and four years later Ricart reached agreement with ENASA to create a powerful sports-racing car as a showcase for Spanish design capability. Naturally, it would be called a Pegaso too. At the heart of this money-no-object project was a double overhead-camshaft alloy V8 engine with supercharging as an option. The Pegaso's strong platform chassis was fitted with a variety of stylish bodies by French and Italian coachbuilders. Still, the competition efforts of the Barcelona-based marque were ill-fated: the two cars entered in the 1953 Le Mans twenty-four-hour race failed to start, and another car caught fire while doing well on the 1954 Carrera PanAmericana. A twin-hull Pegaso record car called 'El Bisiluro' did, however, reach 150.9 mph in a demonstration on a Belgian motorway.

Curiously, the Pegaso car badge – with its 'V8'-suggestive form – embodied a rather less elegant, fatter rendering of Pegasus than that seen on the radiators of Pegaso trucks. Only about a hundred cars were built before the project was halted in

LA VOITURE POUR LES CONNAISSEURS

1958, coincident with Ricart's retirement. Pegaso then concentrated solely on trucks and buses, which it does to this day as part of the IVECO company

PERODUA

A kancil, you may be interested to discover, is a breed of miniature deer native to Malaysia. Featuring in children's stories and folk tales, members of this endangered species grow to the size of small dogs. All of which made the animal an ideal subject for a badge on the second marque of car (after Proton) to emanate from Malaysia.

The first Perodua was built in 1994, to a design licensed from Daihatsu; it was called the Kancil at home and the Nippa for export to right-hand drive markets such as the UK. The deer, seen in silvered profile leaping across a green-backed oval, seemed appropriate on this small urban runabout designed to nip in and out of crowded city streets. It was subsequently attached to the sister Rusa model too.

The emblem, however, was quite different from the Perodua corporate symbol. This was a square coloured in the company's corporate livery of red and green, separated by the thin white outline of the large 'P' with its loop infilled in green too.

In 2000 the gradually expanding company elected to bring its logo on cars and paperwork into line and, maybe, portray a more global image in the new millennium. Hence the badge was redesigned in an elliptical shape, with a far bolder 'P' outline in chrome silver flowing into the oval border. As a corporate logo, this still split the green left-hand side colour from the red on the right, while on cars, such as the recent Kelisa, it simply fronted a black plastic background.

PEUGEOT

The Peugeot empire was partly founded on making items such as pepper mills (below), but the lion trademark denoted the firm's top quality steel; on the current 407 (bottom), the emblem sees its largest-ever application on a production car.

Opposite: this whimsical 2002 Peugeot vehicle concept for a small fire tender was called H2O, partly in reference to its hydrogen power unit; it wore the Peugeot lion symbol on its nose, wheels, doors and circular tailplate.

You can credit Peugeot with a host of motoring achievements: big estate cars, hot hatchbacks, thrifty diesels – indeed, Peugeot is the world's sixth biggest car maker. Its industrial origin, however, was in steel making. In 1810 the Peugeot family of the Sous-Cratet region of eastern France decided to convert their Montbeliard flour mill into a factory making rolled steel. Brothers Jean-Pierre and Jean-Frederic Peugeot set the pace with products made from their own steel, and production and exports boomed. Only nineteen, Jean-Frederic perfected a method of making cheap but high-quality saws, and the business was soon manufacturing clock components, tools, blades, metal stays and hoops for crinoline skirts – and pepper mills, which another Peugeot engineer invented in 1842.

Peugeot realized the value of branding very early on. Someone made the analogy between the strength, the curved back and the extraordinary power of a lion's jaws and the company's fast-selling

saws. In 1847 a Montbeliard goldsmith produced a splendid design for a prowling lion for Peugeot, and from 1850 its saws were all trademarked with it. On 20 November 1858 this became the registered trademark of Peugeot Frères, and despite using other marks for different lines, the lion soon signified the top-notch range made from best-quality cast steel.

Using the big cat may have been given extra patriotic impetus by the nearby town of Belfort. A rampant lion commemorates the town's victory over invading Germans in 1871; this was turned into a coat of arms by the sculptor Frederic-Auguste Bartholdi, who also happened to be responsible for the Statue of Liberty presented to New York by the people of France.

Peugeot's expertise in making metal rods led to the production of bicycle wheel spokes and, by 1885, complete bicycles. It rapidly became France's leading manufacturer of bicycles, and it was not long until the first Peugeot car, designed by Armand Peugeot, took its bow in 1891.

Left: evolution of the lion logo, which first appeared in 1850 stamped on to a saw; below: a Peugeot from about 1903, at a time when the Peugeot family were still not united about the future of the car industry; bottom: the Bébé of 1913 was Peugeot's first mass-market car.

Some members of the dynasty were sceptical of this 15-mph contraption, and it took Armand fourteen years to convince them that it was a moneyspinner. Only in 1905 did the family unite in its faith in the future of car making and allow him to use the hallowed lion logo on the cars' radiator shell, replacing a rectangular and highly decorative Art Nouveau logo that had borne the words 'Automobiles Peugeot' and 'Paris' (from where they were sold).

Nonetheless, Peugeot cars of the 1920s and 1930s generally had a fairly straightforward, landscape-format 'Peugeot' badge on the prow of the radiator shell, and a three-dimensional lion's head and mane as a type of low-lying mascot, the link between the radiator grille top and the chrome strip running along the crest of the bonnet. Later cars of this period had a chrome shield outline in the middle of the radiator grille with 'Peugeot' across the top and model names below such as '301' or '601'.

From being a parochial yet high-quality car manufacturer, after the Second World War Peugeot set out on a steady path of expansion with its 203 model. This was the first to adopt a more Bartholdi-like rampant lion as an upright rectangular bonnet badge. Cars that followed it, including the 403, 404 and 204, sported the image as a gold lion on a large black plastic, chrome-edged shield with 'PEUGEOT' arrayed across the top. The advent of the 504 in 1968 ushered in the era of a free-standing cut-out lion – tongue out, paws in the scratch-your-eyes-out position and surprisingly puny tail flicking in anger – as a silvered-plastic attachment to the radiator grille. A fully chromed 'filled in' version made its debut on the 1996 Peugeot 106, surrounded by a four-sided shape in oblique reference to shields of the past. As a large bonnet emblem on the latest 407, this is now the boldest lion ever seen on a Peugeot car.

The 203 (right), was the first Peugeot to sport the lion image in the basic form still used today; right, centre: three-dimensional lions were commonly used before 1939; far right: chrome-effect and back-printed plastics are the norm on recent cars.

PIERCE-ARROW

America's magnificent 1920s Pierce-Arrow cars (far right and opposite) were generally recognized by their headlamps, which were – unusually for the time – integrated into their mudguards; right: this crest came along in 1928…but left a disastrous legacy.

"There is no mistaking a Pierce-Arrow" ran the slogan of this respected American luxury marque, which made cars between 1901 and 1938. With their unique mudguard-mounted headlights, introduced in 1913, it was true enough.

Another distinctive feature appeared in 1928 on both 81 and 36 series cars: Pierce-Arrow's beautiful 'archer' radiator cap (later bonnet-mounted) mascot. With its helmet and cloak, it was based on a one-off design created by the company ten years previously for opera diva Mary Garden. In 1931 it was updated as a nude by Bonnie Lemm, an artist working for the Ternstedt division of General Motors, the company that supplied the items. She was inspired by Rodin's work but used a reluctant office boy called Albert Gonas to pose for her working sketches.

Until the advent of the archer, frontal identification was provided by a diagonally positioned and handsomely curvaceous 'Pierce' script with a feathered arrow striking it through left to right. It was

witty but rarely seen. More obvious was a hexagonal trademark motif chosen by Pierce-Arrow's art department head, Herbert Dawley: "It is the most attractive of all polygons", he said. It appeared on the ends of the cars' axles and later on hubcaps and spare wheel covers, while a twin-rimmed hexagonal paper trademark had a horizontal arrow across the centre and 'PIERCE' and 'ARROW' arrayed in a circle above and below – the 'ARROW' part shown, incongruously, upside down and therefore back to front.

In the 1920s Dawley left Pierce-Arrow; subsequently his was the first voice ever heard on a TV broadcast, in 1927. Pierce-Arrow must have wished he'd stayed, because in 1928 the firm committed one of the most embarrassing logo mistakes in motoring history. Now owned by Studebaker, Pierce-Arrow introduced a radically new car that year. The Series 81 carried both the new archer mascot and a radiator badge, a gold and red enamelled crest. It had three blue birds

in the main area, two above and one below a red bar, while at the top another blue bird perched on the helmet from a suit of armour. On a scroll beneath it was the Latin motto 'DIXIT ET FECIT', meaning 'he said (it) and he did (it)'.

Pierce-Arrow stated that it was the family crest of company founder George Pierce, a grandson of Dr John Pierce of Axminster, England, the royal physician. George Pierce had died in 1910, but his widow, Louisa, and other family members (none involved with the business any longer) were extremely upset – it wasn't their family crest at all! The resulting acrimony meant that the crest was dropped for 1929 and 1930 models. Cheekily, Pierce-Arrow reinstated a version of this totally inappropriate emblem in 1932, which lasted until the company's sad demise in 1938.

PININFARINA

One of the great car badge riddles is why cars with bodywork designed and/or built by Pininfarina sport a crest with an 'f' on it. The answer lies in the establishment in 1930 of Carrozzeria Pinin Farina, a car bodymaking business founded by a dynamic Italian artisan called Battista Farina, whose family nickname was 'Pinin'. The 'f', with its coiled ascender, stands for his surname. The company and family name was changed to the sonorous compound of Pininfarina in 1961 after a special government decree authorized by Italian president Giovanni Gronchi. This move, unusual in Italy, recognized the tremendous contribution that 'Pinin' Farina had made, both as a design force and as a brand name, to Italy's international reputation as a style leader. Despite Battista Farina's death in 1966, the company has continued to be family-controlled thanks to son Sergio and Sergio's brother-in-law Renzo Carli.

Pininfarina's crest has been in use since the company's very foundation. An upright chrome oblong, the 'f' is in blue and closely surrounded by a thin black keyline. Another black keyline forms an outline frame in which red triangles fit snugly into the top-left and bottom-right corners, giving the impression of the 'f' in a diagonal silver slash. Surmounting this is a dainty crown with four red points and a central pearl-like bead at the very top. The crest is often mounted just aft of the rear wheel arch on Pininfarina-bodied cars; it sits on top of a 'pininfarina' chrome text strip where every letter is joined up along the baseline. This combination dates from around 1950.

As an eighteen-year-old designer working for his brother, Battista Farina's design prowess first came to the fore when he styled the grille for the 1911 Fiat Zero. The output from the company that bears his name has been enormous, but the single car that set the company apart was the Cisitalia 202 of 1947 – deemed so beautiful that the New York Museum of Modern Art instantly added one to its permanent collection.

Its design canon since (and some of these cars have been assembled in Pininfarina's own large factory) has included all-time greats such as the Alfa Romeo Giulietta and Duetto Spiders, Lancia Aurelia B20, Peugeot 403, Austin A40, BMC 1100, Rolls-Royce Camargue, Lancia Gamma coupé, Peugeot 205, Cadillac Allante, Fiat Coupé and even the Hyundai Matrix. Pininfarina bodied its first Ferrari in 1952 and continues to do so today, with the F355 series and Enzo, in a uniquely close-knit relationship. Recent clients have included Ford, which contracted Pininfarina to design, engineer and build its Streetka budget two-seater sports car, and Hafei, a Chinese start-up whose new Lobo city car is being brought from concept to mass-produced item by the company.

pininfarina

PLYMOUTH

Left: apart from a brief spell when its identity was subsumed into that of Chrysler, Plymouth used the Mayflower ship as a talisman during its 73 years; opposite: the marque's badge often found itself overwhelmed by the chrome décor on 1950s Plymouths, such as this 1956/7 example.

In 1928 the Chrysler Corporation introduced two new car brands, Plymouth and DeSoto. De Soto came to the end of its life in 1960, but Plymouth survived until 2001, when DaimlerChrysler decided it had too many marques in its US portfolio and killed it off.

The first Plymouth was an effort to distance the cheaper four-cylinder Chrysler line from the more prestigious six-cylinder Chryslers and Chrysler Imperials. According to a contemporary newspaper article, the Plymouth name was chosen to symbolize "the endurance, strength, the rugged honesty, enterprise, and determination … of the Pilgrim band who were the first American colonists"; they had, of course, set sail from the town of Plymouth, on the south-west tip of England.

Besides the fact that the Pilgrims were not the first American colonialists, it's just as likely that Walter Chrysler picked Plymouth for a similar reason to that behind his choice of the rosette symbol for Chrysler cars: a resonance with prosperous countryfolk. A salesman once asked Chrysler if he'd ever heard of Plymouth brand binder twine, used by farmers for hay baling, and Chrysler responded, "Hell, every farmer's heard of Plymouth binder twine!"

The Pilgrims' ship, the Mayflower, became the white centrepiece of the Plymouth badge in front three-quarters view. 'Plymouth' was written above it in white on a variety of shield- and oval-shaped badges, and, on early cars, 'CHRYSLER MOTORS PRODUCT' was stacked one word above another at the bottom. In 1930 artist Avard Fairbanks came up with a mermaid for the radiator cap mascot to continue the seagoing theme. But she wasn't dressed as a Pilgrim lass: she was bare-breasted, notably buxom and sported wings as well as a tail. It was only fitted for a couple of years.

The ship was incorporated into the yearly changing façade of Plymouths for decades to come, but in the late 1950s Chrysler design chief Virgil Exner, who hated romantic, historical symbols, vetoed the ship emblem; henceforth Plymouths relied on their chrome decoration and 'PLYMOUTH' text nameplates for identity. By the 1980s, indeed, Plymouths generally carried Chrysler's Pentastar logo.

Then, in 1995, Plymouth's ship sailed back into port on a brand new badge. The front half of a ship, sails billowing in the wind, just broke out of a thin white circle to the left, with a dark-blue infill background. An additional dark-blue band around the edge carried 'PLYMOUTH' in its upper hemisphere. That wasn't all, for the hot rod-style Plymouth Prowler two-seater carried a true revival on its pointed nose: a black shield with the Mayflower depiction in silver remarkably like that of the first Plymouths. None of this new-found nostalgia stopped Plymouth from being consigned to history itself, however.

PONTIAC

Opposite: the Torrent SUV takes the Pontiac arrowhead badge into a new market sector; other distinctive Pontiac 'markings' have included John Schinella's 'firebird' artwork (far left), the unique Fiero badge (left), and the marque's original homage to Big Chief Pontiac (centre left).

Pontiac was created in 1926 by General Motors as a companion model line to its Oakland cars. The Oakland plant was in Pontiac, Michigan, which helps explain the straightforward brand derivation. The Pontiac was pitched midway between Chevrolet (with which it shared many components) and Oldsmobile in the GM pecking order, which was based on a mantra, coined by company founder Alfred Sloan, of "a car for every purse". It cost $825. Pontiac was so successful, however, that it had completely eclipsed Oakland by 1932.

The town Pontiac was named after the chief of the Ottawa Indians, who led the rebellion of 1763–64 in which the whole western frontier rose up against British colonialists – only to be defeated because the French refused to support him. The earliest Pontiac radiator badge, therefore, featured two slightly overlapping circles as two sides of a silver coin. One contained a cameo profile of the Indian chief with 'PONTIAC' arrayed around the top and

'CHIEF OF THE SIXES' around the bottom – referring to Pontiac's concentration, until 1932, on six-cylinder engines. The flipside of the coin featured the statement 'PRODUCT OF GENERAL MOTORS' and a laurel wreath to enhance it. In 1929 the cars underwent a redesign, acquiring a bonnet ornament in the shape of Pontiac's head and a 'Pontiac' script on the radiator grille. A few years later the logo was redefined in red (and often positioned on the bonnet sides) as a silhouette profile of Pontiac with a streamlined feather headdress in a circle.

What Chief Pontiac's descendants thought about his image being used to sell cars is unknown. As minority rights rose in importance in US politics in the 1950s, however, it may have been considered politically incorrect. In any case, the final Indian chief hood mascot had been deleted by 1957, and in 1959 there was a complete logo change. The wide, low and long 1959-model Pontiacs now sported a red arrowhead or dart – downwards-pointing, and edged in chrome – with a

four-pointed star at the top.

Pontiac presented an increasingly sporty image in the 1960s, including inventing the 'muscle car' in 1964 with the powerful GTO model. In its pursuit of machismo power, in 1973 it launched a secondary powerful image on the Firebird Trans-Am – the so-called 'screaming chicken' – an enormous bonnet decal showing an eagle with flames surging from its outstretched feathers. The artwork was by Pontiac stylist John Schinella. In 1983 Pontiac adopted a new motto, 'We Build Excitement', and proved it in 1984 when it launched the Fiero, the first mid-engined sports car from a mainstream US car maker. This had its own unique bonnet badge, a black-backed shield with 'Fiero' across the top and the blazing eagle, with wings thrust upwards, both in reddish gold. Today's Pontiacs continue to display the red arrowhead logo, which is as dynamic and thrusting as some of its cars, particularly the new Solstice two-seater roadster.

PORSCHE

The cars might get more outrageous, such as the Carrera GT roadster (opposite), but the Porsche badge remains a constant; the Boxster (right) has been a big hit for Porsche; bottom: Porsche's timeless corporate script gazes down on an early 356, 917 racer and Cayenne 4x4.

Suggest prancing black horses and sports cars, and even the least well-informed people immediately summon up Ferrari's famous image. Yet the greatest sports car marque in German motoring history – Porsche – also uses just such a creature on its cars, as part of its never-changing badge. The badge first appeared on the centre of the steering wheel of the dainty Porsche 356A in 1953, and it is barely changed on today's cars, such as the Boxster, 911 and Cayenne.

The Porsche 356 grew out of Dr Ferdinand Porsche's brilliant design work on the Volkswagen Beetle. It was intended to be "the perfect weekend sports car" based on the rock-solid mechanical elements of the Beetle itself. Porsche died in 1951 when the Porsche 356 had barely reached its first customers, yet his son (also Ferdinand, but always known as Ferry) was responsible for the car's creation and development and with consistency, rigour and steadiness turned the company into a major success. The 911 of 1963 was the car

that really made Porsche's name; it is deeply desired to this day in its modern incarnation, which still relies on a rear-mounted six-cylinder engine.

The Porsche company was founded in Stuttgart in 1931, decamped to Austria in 1944, but returned to Stuttgart in 1950 to begin car manufacture. It adopted Stuttgart's own coat of arms as its badge. In the Middle Ages, Stuttgart was the site of a stud farm (the meaning of the name itself) in the long-gone dukedom Württemburg. The Porsche badge, therefore, is a shield within a shield. In the centre is the smaller, yellow-backed one with 'STUTTGART' and a rearing black horse enamelled in black. The bigger shield, meanwhile, is divided into quarters: top-left and bottom-right each carry three stags' antlers in gold; their opposite numbers have two red and two black horizontal, alternating stripes. These elements represent the coat of arms of the Baden-Württemburg region of which Stuttgart is the capital, but across the top the word 'PORSCHE' is engraved in the gold

base colour of the badge.

The badge has been used ever since, including on the Cayenne, which is Porsche's entry into the fast-expanding sport-utility vehicle market. However, almost as familiar is the 'PORSCHE' text, a highly individual rendering in red, laterally elongated, square-cut capitals, which has been seen on company communications since the very start. Both badge and text are paragons of continuity, something all Porsche enthusiasts cherish.

PROTON

Proton's previous logo (left) saluted Malaysia's thirteen former states, but gave way to a new badge on cars such as the Satria (opposite) featuring a golden tiger below: the first Proton, the Saga, whose badge risked offence to Christian sensibilities.

Malaysia had never had an indigenous car marque before Proton came along in 1985. Backed by the Malaysian government, the early Protons were effectively licence-built Mitsubishi Lancers, and the fact that Malaysia drives on the left quickly turned Britain into Proton's largest export market for the right-hand drive cars.

An initial shipment of sample evaluation cars, however, caused mild concern among those charged with marketing them. It was actually the badge that was at issue. An upright chrome diamond with an elongated lower point was the background for a black, lozenge-like diamond logo. The main part of this was a yellow and silver star with fourteen points, representing the thirteen former states of federal Malaya that had been joined together to make up the modern Malaysia, plus one extra for Malaysia itself. A silver sickle moon crescent curled around the underneath of this, signifying the Islamic faith prevalent in Malaysia. It was this religious symbol, thought some,

that might have upset British sensibilities, and when the cars went on full sale in 1989 the badge featured only the star.

Proton went for a logo revamp in 2000, finally ditching its fourteen-pointed star. The new Proton badge was shield-shaped, edged in gold with a matching gold 'PROTON', and with a dark-blue infill colour. In a dark-green circle in the centre was a stylized gold tiger's head. The big cat is Malaysia's national symbol in the way that Britain has its bulldog, and the green colour apparently signified the respect the country has for its lush rainforests.

Proton now also develops its own cars from scratch, such as the Waja/Impian and new Gen2 family hatchback; it also owns Britain's Lotus sports car marque and engineering consultancy.

RELIANT

Reliant has been one of the keenest exponents of the unfashionable three-wheeled motoring format, having built over two hundred thousand of such vehicles between 1935 and 2000. Its location in the Black Country, the British West Midlands area synonymous with mining and the Industrial Revolution, had a crucial bearing on its sales: many Reliant owners were miners – latterly, ex-miners – who owned a Reliant car because they once rode to work on a motorcycle; Reliants could be driven in the UK on a motorbike licence.

The first Reliant cars, rather than vans, arrived in 1952, and sported a bizarre little bonnet mascot, its two stems held on by bolts and, in profile, looking like a trailing comet with the skeletal image of three circles – mirroring the three-wheel theme – framed within it. The all-new Regal 3/25 of 1962 swapped this for a triangular bonnet badge split by a three-pointed star into three sections, each with an 'R' revolving around the centre. The background was

white with a further triangular shape in dark-blue at the centre. While hardly glamorous, fifty thousand Regals were sold, their popularity boosted by the early 1970s fuel crisis.

Its replacement, the 1974 Robin, came with a new badge. Now a triangular shield, it had a chrome outer edge, an inner red keyline and 'RELIANT' in silver in a band across the top. Below that was a generic castle image with two turrets, and the background was dark-blue. The Robin's replacement, the 1982 Rialto, had simply a 'RELIANT' nameplate. In 1990 the company came up with a much more aggressive logo: the word 'RELIANT' was backed by a geometric rendering of an eagle with its wings outspread behind the nameplate. It was generally applied in silver with a black background.

All of this overlooks Reliant's other activity: sports cars. It made a real splash with the Scimitar GTE in 1968, the world's first sports estate car. On its bonnet, as on the Scimitar SS1 sports car of 1984, a narrow

black shield came with the gold image of a scimitar sword with its blade pointing downwards.

Regrettably for those who celebrate automotive biodiversity, none of these interesting alternative vehicles made it into the twenty-first century as Reliant abandoned car manufacture in 2000.

65

miles
per
gallon

in a family car

The
**new
3/25**

REG 325

Reliant

RENAULT

The badge on the Renault Scenic (opposite) is part of the bold design front the French company today presents, and is a long way removed from the 1920s days, below, wher the 'badge' was actually a conduit to emit the sound of the horn.

Louis Renault built his first car in his parents' back garden in Paris; he put it into production in 1898, but only thanks to financial backing from his brother Marcel. This family partnership was saluted in 1900 with the introduction of the firm's first badge, an agreeable if somewhat bland Art Nouveau trademark featuring two intricate 'R's mirroring one another – to represent siblings Louis and Marcel, of course – in an oval with a floral garland above it.

In 1906 a more dynamic new badge featured the head-on image of a Renault racing car with its characteristically shaped bonnet encircled in a graphic representation of a gear wheel. In 1919 this was replaced by another circular motif, this time depicting a somewhat cartoonish image of a tank. The now familiar diamond-shaped emblem appeared in 1925, at first with the 'RENAULT' name set across a slatted centre section. This device was initially intended simply to allow the sound of the car's novel electric horn to

be emitted, which was sited just behind it; it replaced a circular grille with a similar function that had been introduced just two years before.

The firm was nationalized by the French government in 1945, just a year after Louis Renault died in prison, where he was being held under suspicion of collaborating with the occupying Nazi forces. The popular Renault 4CV continued to wear the Renault badge on a fake radiator grille of three chrome bars (the car was actually rear-engined), but its 1956 successor, the Dauphine, bizarrely ditched the familiar logo in favour of a shield-shaped badge, showing a black background peppered by small red diamonds, with a gold crown on it. At the top was written 'RENAULT REGIE NATIONALE' in red, and below the crown was 'FRANCE' in gold. Odd, somehow, that a nationalized company in a republic would promote imagery reflecting the former French royal family.

This Renault diamond badge grew simpler as the years wore on; it was often

applied in a jaunty, off-set position on top-selling models such as the Renault 4 and 8. The 'RENAULT' lettering was discarded in 1972 in an attempt to make the badge appear both simpler and more three-dimensional. At this time, the keynote yellow colour of Renault badges changed to a suitably trendy 1970s orange. This had the predictable effect of dating very quickly, but it was not until 1992 that Renault had a proper rethink. The new badge was still a diamond, but this time depicted on paper as a towering monolith, uplit and displayed from a worm's-eye-view perspective. The car badge itself, finished in chrome, was designed to slope up to and down from a centre crease point to reflect natural light, so it truly stood out when bolted to a bonnet or boot lid. The corporate colour change in 1992 was to a vivid yellow, which was toned down once again in 2004.

Right: a 40CV was an early proponent of the Renault diamond; below: the badge offset on the Renault 10 (left), and 4 (right); right, top: regal pretensions for the Renault Dauphine. Opposite: the 1996 Renault Fiftie concept car.

RILEY

Modern car drivers might not know it, but the Riley name was seen on a range of 1930s sports cars and sporting saloons that rivalled Alfa Romeo for performance and style. The Riley Cycle Company was founded in 1896 and built its first four-wheeled car in 1906 after making a name for itself with powered tricycles. By 1911 Riley had formed a new car-making company in Coventry, England, but it was at the 1919 Olympia Motor Show in London that the now familiar blue diamond-shaped badge was first revealed, on the radiator of the four-cylinder Riley Eleven.

The diamond was horizontally orientated, with 'Riley' expressed in a 'joined-up' handwriting style, the 'R' beginning with two curved strokes and the 'y' terminating in a looped ascender that curled around and back on itself under the rest of the word. The outline and lettering was in polished metal and the background infill was dark-blue enamel. The emblem itself was curved to match the pointed prow of the Riley radiator grille on

pretty cars such as the Sprite and Kestrel.

Riley (acquired by Morris in 1938) launched one of the best-loved British sports saloons of the post-war period in the RM series, introduced in 1945. These cars feature one of the few significant variations in Riley badges: the 1.5-litre models carry the traditional dark-blue badge, while 2.5-litre models have a light-blue version. Both are chromed.

After these fine cars, however, the Riley badge was used to denote upmarket Austin/Morris cars. It seems, in retrospect, a scandalous waste of a brand name with a terrific reputation; some of the final cars used a cheap aluminium badge with Riley printed on it rather than enamelled. The very last Riley car, a 4/72 saloon, was built in 1969, since when the name has remained dormant, latterly in a folder in Munich. Via its stewardship of the Rover Group between 1994 and 2000, BMW now owns the Riley name, and it came very close to being revived on a version of the Rover 75 in 1999. Sadly, it was not to be.

ROLLS-ROYCE

In a world where international air travel is now within the reach of tens of millions of 'ordinary' people, the Rolls-Royce logo is most familiar from its prominent position on jet engines – a sign of reliability and power. Indeed, the trademark is owned by Rolls-Royce plc, a world-leading aero engine manufacturer, and used under licence by Rolls-Royce Motor Cars; the two divisions of the British company were separated in 1971, and BMW now owns the car side.

Of course, the Rolls-Royce car is just as famous, yet in an entirely different way – declared the "best car in the world" by a journalist on *The Times* in London, writing in 1908, and, in terms of magnificence and quality, more than living up to that accolade for a hundred years. The company was formed by Henry Royce and the Hon. Charles Rolls in 1904 to build cars; Rolls-Royce's radiator badge was first used in 1906 on the Silver Ghost: an upright rectangle with intertwined 'R's in the centre, 'ROLLS' at the top and 'ROYCE' at the bottom, the three sections framed in

keylines and these, plus the lettering, in red enamel. It is not recorded whether it was the personal creation of either Rolls or Royce.

In late 1930 the red was changed to black. An internal memo dated 18 December 1930 reads: "The radiator medallion is filled in red, and this is generally the only red on the car. Artistically this may, and often is, considered to be wrong. On R's (Royce's) car – 27EX – we filled it in black, since black is on most cars and is no colour at all, and therefore does not clash with any colour. Could we not standardize a black fitting?"

The response was: "To inform you that we have been considering the black medallion and decided some days ago to adopt this for the front of the radiator on the 40/50hp and to leave it red on the 20/25hp as one of the few external distinguishing features between the two, and the works have already been instructed accordingly." In the event, all cars were in fact changed to black.

The changing image of Rolls-Royce (left, from top to bottom): the 1928 16EX experimental car; the 1904 10 hp model that heralded Rolls-Royce car manufacture in 1904; and the 1963 Silver Cloud II that, for many, is still the definitive Rolls-Royce form.

Theories that they were changed to black as a mark of respect after Sir Henry Royce's death in 1933 are untrue.

Red badges have reappeared three times, however: in 1979 on a run of 225 Silver Shadow IIs to celebrate Rolls-Royce's seventy-fifth anniversary; in 2002 on the final Silver Seraph and Corniche models built in a factory at Crewe, Cheshire; and on thirty-five Phantoms in 2004 to commemorate the Rolls-Royce centenary. The only other changes have been a reduction in overall size in 1996, and on the 1998 Silver Seraph the deletion of the serifs on the words 'ROLLS' and 'ROYCE' (but not the 'RR' monogram).

Just as famous as the badge is the Rolls-Royce radiator mascot. By 1910 Henry Royce had become concerned about the craze for attaching comical mascots to car radiators, especially the grotesque black cats, policemen and small devils that some Rolls-Royce owners had adopted. He despised mascots but, bowing to demand, agreed to an 'official'

Rolls-Royce one to put a stop to the practice, providing it was worthy of one of his cars.

John Scott Montagu, an English aristocrat and friend of Charles Rolls, had arranged for artist Charles Sykes, who worked on Montagu's own motoring magazine, to illustrate the 1911 Rolls-Royce sales catalogue. Now the company commissioned Sykes to sculpt a mascot that would both demonstrate the cars' qualities and enhance their overall look. He came up with the figurine of a girl with arms outstretched holding the folds of her gown blowing in the breeze.

Sykes used John Montagu's secretary, Eleanor Thornton, as the model for his work which he completed on 16 February 1911, and once the design was agreed upon, she was famous for ever. The mascot became known as 'The Flying Lady' or 'The Silver Lady'; its correct title, however, is 'The Spirit of Ecstasy'. With several variations, it has been a fixture on all Rolls-Royce cars from 1911 to today.

The contemporary Rolls-Royce Phantom positively drips with logos; neat touches include a weighted wheel hub logo that remains upright at all times (far left) and an engraved logo on the handle of the pull-out umbrella concealed in the door (left).

HX03 BWG

ROVER

Thanks to its troubled involvement with British Leyland and its successors from 1968, the Rover Viking ship badge has made an appearance on an extraordinary variety of cars. It is, though, perhaps best known as the emblem adorning a long line of medium-sized saloons with a premium quality feel and plenty of power; a Rover car in this vein has been available constantly from the mid-1930s to today.

The logo first appeared as a radiator badge in 1929, twenty-four years after the former Rover Cycle Company of Coventry, England, had turned to car making. It began as a bicycle manufacturer in 1905, company founder John Kemp Starley inventing the 'Safety Cycle', the design of which has inspired almost every bicycle since. How many Chinese pedallers know that? It was later marketed as a 'Rover' simply because it was intended for roving around on.

Early cars made do with a variety of flowing renderings of the 'ROVER' name

attached to the radiator grille. Then, in 1921, a catalogue featured a picture of a Viking ship, for the first time associating Rover cars with the world's most formidable roving people, the Scandinavian conquerors of the eighth, ninth and tenth centuries. In 1922 a figurine of a Viking holding a shield and battle-axe was offered as a radiator cap ornament for Rover cars, for the price of £1 (in 1924, the Rover 9 car cost £215).

By 1929 the Viking theme was fully adopted on production cars. Radiator caps featured a helmeted Viking head mascot, while an enamelled radiator badge showed a black Viking longship with the figurehead of a Viking warrior on its prow; the bows of the boat were cutting waves through a blue sea, and 'ROVER' was spelt out on the sail. By 1930 Rover had registered this as its trademark.

Variations on the theme occurred as the badge evolved in tandem with Rover's cars. For example, the Viking head at one time became a separate entity in chrome

The first Rover 'Viking' was a radiator mascot accessory (left), but in 1929 the design seen above became standard fitment.

Rover's early shield-shaped grille surround (right) exerted a heavy influence on the later badge shape, as shown (opposite) on the 1999 Rover 25.

relief above the badge; the waves were redrawn to make them more realistic and less like huge leaves; the ship became gold on a black background; and the sail of the boat was coloured maroon. In 1936 an inverted pear shape was used to frame the image, and this became a feature of each successive Rover, sitting at the top of a central chrome stem fronting the radiator grille and with model names such as '60', '75' and '100' incorporated into it. Rarely has a car badge been altered as many times as Rover's Viking ship – there were more than a dozen variations.

With the launch of the Rover P6 2000 in 1963, the largest ever rendition appeared. 'ROVER' was now detailed separately above the sail in the black area of sky; a later variant of the car also carried a skeletal version, in simplified outline. The 1967 P5B coupé, meanwhile, had an even more austere version in gold finish, barely recognizable at all as a vessel, and an only moderately less abstract version graced the SD1 3500 in 1976. However, a richly executed rendering of the Viking ship – gold boat, black background, red sail and all – on a broad shield returned in 1979.

Not all Rovers since have been convincing bearers of the badge, particularly rebranded versions of the Austin Metro and Montego. However, since a management buy-out of Rover from BMW in 2000, the badge has appeared on some interesting cars, especially the latest Rover 75 V8. In 2004, moreover, after a twenty-five-year period of sticking to the elaborate Viking badge tradition, Rover opted for a simpler rendition again. The new badge has a plain red sail; no oars, Viking masthead or waves; and a generally less heritage-laden aura.

Sadly, the company went into receivership in 2005.

SAAB

Today's Saabs have an eye-catching badge: it's a gleaming, domed, plastic medallion in lustrous dark-blue with two silver rings around the edge. The focal point, occupying the centre and upper areas, is the profile image of a griffin, an imaginary half-lion-half-eagle beast red-edged in silver, its tongue aggressively poking out, and wearing a three-pronged crown. Underneath it, 'SAAB' is spelt out, the four characters merging together at the baseline.

All well and good, you might think, but this isn't really Saab's badge at all. It belongs to Scania, a Swedish truck maker, and its position on Saab cars reflects the relative importance of the two companies.

Svenska Aeroplan AB (the Swedish Aircraft Company) revealed its small car prototype in 1947 and put a revised version on sale in 1949, calling it the Saab 92. Its two-stroke three-cylinder engine, front-wheel drive and aerodynamic styling made it popular, as did the Saab's sturdiness, but the bonnet-mounted badge was pretty dull: 'SAAB' in a circle, both in shiny bare metal. However, the Model 92B in 1952 added a little character to its livery: a squareish badge framed 'SAAB', all in bare metal, while a chrome bar sticking out on either side made it look like the head-on image of an aircraft. It was soon rendered in black on silver.

On later cars the badge descended to the radiator grille itself, initially being reinterpreted as simply a metal outline of 'SAAB', but eventually having the letters fanned out above a head-on image of a 1941 Saab B18 military aircraft, its spinning propellers represented by two rings around its engines. The work of Olaf Norelius, it was seen on the Saab 99 in 1967, a much-loved car that started to build Saab's excellent reputation for occupant safety; it was also seen as a 'solid' badge with a mid-blue background on the Saab 94, which now had a V4 Ford engine. In 1973, however, this attractive design was dropped, and for fourteen years Saabs carried nothing more than a textual

Addo
SVEA NORNAN
JORDBRUKSKASSAN
GLASÖGONHUSET
för god mat
GULINS
RKADEN
SAAB 93

nameplate. The 99 Turbo of 1977, Europe's first proper turbocharged production car, sported a distinctive 'TURBO' identity, the 'O' of the word segmented to represent the vanes on its turbocharger fan.

In 1987 Saabs gained a new bonnet badge, designed by Carl Fredrik Reutersward. It was the griffin's debut on a Saab, a move to reflect the car division's merger with Scania to form the Saab Scania Group within Saab. Above the griffin it read 'SAAB'; below it 'SCANIA'. Mr Reutersward described his work thus: "The symbol consists of a roundel inscribed with two circles, transposed to form a cylindrical band and create an impression of optical movement. Although each is shown in its own perspective, Saab and Scania are seen as a unit."

In fact this was the logo of the highly profitable Scania truck company, which was imposed on the loss-making Saab car operation; the griffin comes from the crest for the Skane district of southern Sweden, where Scania is based. Shortly after

America's General Motors took full control of Saab Automobile in 2000, Saab's badge was changed to that still current today, losing the Scania word but, bizarrely, keeping its emblem. Since then, the Saab badge has made an appearance on the first car that is neither made nor designed by Saab, the 9-2. This is a five-door Subaru Impreza with Saab touches, which is intended to help lift the fortunes of the still loss-making Saab. Interestingly, GM now has two brands using the griffin as a logo – Saab and Vauxhall – but aircraft imagery is creeping back to Saab: the 2003 9-3 SportHatch concept incorporated the head-on aircraft form as the handle to lift the boot floor cover.

SATURN

The Saturn division of General Motors was formed with one clear aim: to counter the influx of excellent quality Japanese small car imports with something better, unusual and American. Yet its choice of name and logo was, rather bizarrely, rooted in a different confrontation – the Cold War. Phil Garcia, chief designer at GM's Advanced Design Studio, is credited with suggesting the 'Saturn' name; he was inspired by the Saturn rocket that carried Americans to the moon during the space race with the USSR. In July 1982 Saturn was selected as the codename for the project, but after it was publicly announced in November 1983 by GM chairman Roger Smith and president F. James McDonald, it inevitably became the marque name too.

In December 1987 Saturn unveiled its new corporate logo. It was a section of the ringed planet in a stylized form on a bright red background square. 'SATURN' was spelt out below, in a neutral grey on chrome. Its rise to American familiarity began in February 1989 when the first Saturn advertisement appeared, shortly before the cars went on sale.

The Saturn project took a 'ground zero' approach, creating a new car and a completely new plant in Tennessee to build it. It was a huge gamble for GM, which kept its distance so that Saturn wouldn't be tainted with any preconceived motor industry thinking or practices. But the sensible Saturn cars and direct customer approach proved a hit: in March 1992 Saturn produced its 100,000th car and, in June 1995, built its millionth – a dark-green SC2 coupé. It rolled off the line bedecked with a banner reading "What are the odds?!" Right-hand drive Saturns have also been a success in the heart of 'enemy' territory – Japan.

In the last few years Saturn's badge has dropped the 'SATURN' wording, making room to display the square planet image even more prominently. This is in line with an expansion of the product into bolder, less resolutely suburban areas such as sport-utility vehicles.

SEAT

The serrated 'S' badge is growing ever more prominent on new Seats, especially now that the Spanish brand has a bold new grille design in which to display it; the cars have come a long way since the days when the company was a purveyor of locally made Fiats.

The bold chrome 'S' on Seats has been around since 1998. Two diagonal black lines strike through the central curve of the letter, while the character itself appears highly compressed, the usual open spaces almost squeezed out. It is a refinement of the style first seen on the 1980 Seat Ronda. Then, the middle curve of the 'S' split into five thin chrome strips, meshing with five black plastic ones from the left. This 'S' design was repeated in the company's corporate nameplate. Both were revised in 1992 with four chrome and four black strips. With the 1998 revamp came not only a new colour for the text, blue instead of red and silver, but also a touch of style for the 'A', with its top right corner chiselled off, avoiding any confusion with the letter 'R'.

Seat was an acronym for Sociedad Española de Automoviles de Turismo (Spanish Passenger Car Company). Its first car, in 1953, was a licence-built Fiat 1400, and its badge, designed to fit where Fiat's own would have been found, made no secret of this. A shield-shaped centre section carried the 'SEAT' name in elongated capitals, with the canted 'A' mirroring 'FIAT's own letter in the very same position, while a banner below this read 'LICENCIA FIAT'; the text and surround was in silver chrome, the infill red enamel. Either side, aircraft-style wings tapered to a point, while surrounding the shield were two more chrome wings in the manner of a bird of prey just about to carry off some unfortunate small mammal.

Seat put Spain on wheels with its licence-built Fiat 600. Its cars briefly adopted a Fiat-style roundel, complete with laurel garland, in 1968, but in 1970 the company ditched a conventional badge altogether, plumping for four square-cut 'S-E-A-T' capitals, each in an identical black square in a uniform line. By 1980 Seat was disenchanted in its relationship with Fiat, eventually severing its connections and designing its first completely independent model, the Ibiza, in 1984. Two years later Volkswagen bought a controlling stake, eventually acquiring the whole of Seat.

SHELBY

The Cobra (a 427 model is shown opposite) was the creation of Texan Carroll Shelby, who took the imagery of the snake and turned it into a logo as fearsome as the cars' electric performance; copies are numerous, and disputes over the protection of the Cobra design and name seemingly ongoing.

Carroll Shelby, now in his eighties, was the racing driver from Texas who created the Cobra phenomenon. The powerful two-seater sports-racing cars were sold under the marque name Shelby between 1962 and 1968, and just over one thousand of these beautiful Anglo-American machines were produced. However, the desire of the impecunious to own one has turned the Cobra into the most copied car in history, with dozens of different lookalikes outnumbering originals by maybe a hundred to one.

Shelby had the idea for the Cobra in 1960, when he decided to create an American sports car using one of the light and powerful V8 engines manufactured in Detroit. Eventually, to save costs, he settled upon the cocktail of Britain's attractive AC Ace, with a redesigned chassis frame and a small-block Ford V8 engine. In 1962 the production body/chassis was air-freighted from AC Cars in the UK to his new Californian workshop, where the engine was fitted and the car burst into fire-breathing life. "It only took about eight hours to fit", recalled Shelby. "We painted the name 'Shelby' on the front. Soon after that, we came up with the Cobra name. The car became known as the Shelby Cobra or, to give credit to everyone, the Shelby AC Cobra, powered by Ford."

A badge was created, a chrome-edged circle with a red outer band linking to a red bar across the circle, one third of the way up from the base, on which 'COBRA' was depicted in chrome show-through letters. In the two-part central area was the fearsome depiction of a cobra snake, rearing and ready to attack, on a white enamel background.

The first of hundreds of race victories for the Cobra was at Riverside in 1963; the even more powerful Cobra 427 won at such events as Sebring, Brands Hatch and Le Mans. In 1965 Shelby American came back to Europe and won the FIA world championship with the Cobra Daytona coupé. The first Cobra was a road sensation, too: *Sports Car Graphic*

magazine recorded 0–60 mph in 4.1 seconds.

In 1965 ownership of the Cobra name passed to Ford after a lucrative sponsorship deal with Shelby. Since the original Cobra ceased manufacture in 1968, Carroll Shelby has been involved in several revivals, and uses the Cobra name and badge under licence from Ford. Together, he and Ford continue to fight against pirate cars and the often flagrant appropriation of the Cobra name for them.

SIMCA

Simca used the old French word for swallow, Aronde, as the name for its popular 1954 family car, shown below and bottom.

A very striking evocation of the bird was the company's corporate symbol, opposite, on both factory insignia and on the cars themselves – you can see it here on the hubcaps of this Simca 1300.

This acronym stands for Société Industrielle de Mécanique et Carrosserie Automobile (the Automobile Engine and Bodywork Manufacturing Company). It was a French company, founded in 1926 to import Fiats, which in 1936 turned to assembling the Italian cars under licence as well.

The cars became increasingly French with the launch in 1946 of the Simca 6. It carried Simca's new badge, an upright rectangular shield with a tiny pointed tip on its bottom horizontal edge. Split 60/40 into a mid-blue section at the top with a bright red section below, 'SIMCA' in slightly elongated white letters was in the lower half while the upper half carried an abstract rendering of a swallow seen from below (or above – it's hard to tell) in flight. The inference was that Simca sipped fuel, and glided like a bird.

The badge, in fact, was to heavily influence the cars because in 1951 Simca launched the Aronde, the old French word for 'swallow'. In the 1960s the corporate logo was modified, appearing on dealer signage and advertising but no longer being found on the front of Simca cars. The swallow part was changed so that the bird was now seen in extremely abstract form from the side, launching itself into the air; this detail alone was used on such cars as the Simca 1300 and 1500 of 1963, on their chrome hubcaps.

Even that little motif was eradicated from Simcas by 1966. Chrysler had taken the company over in 1963, and Simca livery rapidly became nothing more than the word itself, either as individually attached chrome letters or as 'SIMCA' on an oblong nameplate. However, in contrast to its Hillman, Humber and Sunbeam brands in the UK, which were transformed into Chryslers in 1976, the American company gave Simca a stay of execution, and it lasted until 1980 – without its badge!

SKODA

The Skoda logo was used as a free-standing metal mascot on this Superb model of 1938 (right, top), but by the time of the final 'Communist-era' model, the 1989 Favorit (right, below), it was a cheap plastic emblem, fitted offset; opposite: the Skoda Yeti concept.

Skoda's green-and-black badge has an interesting history. It was created between 1915 and 1920 by the commercial director of the Skoda company in Pilsen, Czechoslovakia, who wanted a new logo for the armaments and machine tool firm. A stylized representation of an Indian headdress with feathers and an arrow, it is believed to be inspired by a native American family servant. It was registered as a trademark on 15 December 1923.

Two years later Skoda merged with car manufacturer Laurin & Klement. This company's founders began by making bicycles in 1895, initially called Slavias but renaming them Laurin & Klements in 1904. Their 1905 catalogue included their first car, the Voituretta. This bore the 'L&K' initials in a circle garlanded with laurel leaves in an Art Nouveau style; the laurel leaves are thought to be a play on the name Laurin, the engineering brains behind the cars.

For 1925, the cars carried both Laurin & Klement and Skoda identities, while in 1926 they carried the 'SKODA' name in a blue-enamelled badge still edged with Laurin's leaves. After that they adopted the feathered Skoda emblem as a bonnet mascot, in both a front-on and side-on version, the latter with a streamlined chrome tail on cars such as the popular Rapid and luxury Superb of the late 1930s.

The curious little design has proved incredibly durable, worn by most Skoda cars during the company's post-war Communist era. By the late 1960s it was an enamel badge in white with a red background, although by the 1980s it was a cheap-looking black plastic moulding with silver detail. On the initial versions of the front-wheel drive 1989 Favorit, the pivotal model that led to Skoda being acquired by Volkswagen, the badge was offset to the left on the car's sloping nose.

VW has proved an excellent custodian of the company, now in the Czech Republic, with its complex heritage. In 1995 it rolled out a new version of the Skoda badge on the Felicia. On a black background, the head-dress motif is in a mid-green; 'SKODA' curves around the top, while in the lower orbit a semicircular garland once more recalls Mr Laurin's input. Detail, text and keylines are in silver, while a corporate paper trademark adopts the same design but substitutes 'AUTO' for the leaves.

VW has read new meaning in to the badge: the outer circle represents global production and sales, the wing technical progress, and the arrow advancement and quality. The arrow's 'eye' represents vision, precision and technical awareness.

SMART

By the late 1990s the creation of an all-new mainstream marque, with its own all-new logo/badge, was an extremely rare event. This happened with 'Smart', however, which came into being in 1997. Besides being a catchy word in itself, Smart concealed a secret message.

The 'S' stood for Swatch, the Swiss watchmaker formed by Nicolas Hayek, who instigated this project for an ultra-compact two-seater city car that aimed to add the elusive element of fun to urban driving. The 'm', meanwhile, stood for Mercedes-Benz, Mr Hayek's partner in the venture (the German car maker initially held an 81% share in the Micro Compact Car (MCC) enterprise, but has since taken it over entirely). The 'art' part, asserts the brand today, speaks for itself, for the Fortwo two-seater has certainly redrawn the motoring map like no other tiny city car. It has made super-economical motoring hip.

Brand recognition had to be achieved in double-quick time. However, although the marque was officially MCC, it was 'smart' that was spelt out on the stubby nose of the City-Coupé in 1997 in decal form, all in light-grey lower case with the 'a' featuring a triangular yellow cursor-like detail on its upper loop.

In September 2002 MCC was renamed simply as Smart, and the logo changed, as the brand embarked on a product expansion to include a sports car and a four-door model. It was a rearrangement of familiar elements: as a bonnet badge, Smart's cars adopted the 'pictogram' of a circle whose right-hand side was formed of a triangular arrow pointing outwards. It had a brushed aluminium finish. On the tail, the word 'smart' was spelt out as a grey decal but now without its yellow arrow. On paperwork and signage – but not on the characterful cars themselves – the symbol was shown in grey with a yellow arrow and the 'smart' word in matching grey.

SPYKER

The Dutch Spyker C8 supercar, introduced in 2001, carries a splendid and evocative badge. The principal image is of a wire wheel clad with a tyre. Ranging round the upper semicircle of the tyre is 'SPYKER', while on the corresponding lower half is a Latin motto: 'NULLA TENACI INVIA EST VIA' – 'for the tenacious no road is impassable'. Then, seemingly fixed to the wheel hub, the propeller of a vintage aeroplane breaks out on either side of the round image.

The Spyker C8 Spyder was unveiled at the British motor show in 2000, a dramatic mid-engined two-seater with an Audi V8 engine and a handbuilt cockpit. It revived a name that was last seen in 1925, when the original Spyker was liquidated. Also a Dutch firm, the Spyker marque was formed in 1900 by brothers Jacobus and Hendrik-Jan Spijker. These former coachbuilders used the Spyker name on their cars for better recognition in foreign markets, and placed a brass 'Spyker' nameplate on the cars' circular radiator grille mesh, in a squiggly handwritten style, to prove it.

The company was taken over by a business consortium during the First World War, when it diversified into aircraft. A new car, the C1, was designed in 1916, and was the first Spyker to carry the new wheel/propeller badge, which was designed by Spyker director Henri Wijnmalen to reflect the company's dual focus. It was always fitted as a purely chromed emblem. The badge was also worn by the excellent Maybach-engined C4 in 1920. It was widely regarded as Holland's answer to Rolls-Royce, but only 150 were sold, and its inability to boost Spyker's turnover led to bankruptcy.

Production at the new Spyker works, however, is running at about twenty-five cars a year, which ensures exclusivity; as a nod to Spyker's fighter aircraft heritage, each one comes with a leather flying jacket hand-tailored to the intrepid customer.

SSANGYONG

Will the takeover of South Korean car maker SsangYong prove prophetic? In November 2004 the Seoul-based 4x4 vehicle specialist signed an agreement with China's state-owned Shanghai Automotive Industry Corp (SAIC), leading to its taking a commanding stake. Dry financial detail in itself, but highly significant because it means that SsangYong is the first existing manufacturer to be taken over by a Chinese company.

SsangYong's shaky start mirrors the hesitant but determined beginnings of many Chinese manufacturers now. The SsangYong conglomerate entered the car industry in 1988 with the Korando range (standing for 'Koreans Can Do', no less, while SsangYong means 'two dragons'), off-road vehicles that were close copies of the Jeep CJ and Mitsubishi Shogun. They carried a 'SSANGYONG' text nameplate only.

In 1993, however, the company launched its first independently developed car, the Musso. It carried

SsangYong's new car badge, the work of British design consultants John Heffernan and Ken Greenley – the latter also created the Musso's styling. Attached to the centre of the radiator grille, a large-diameter, thin-rimmed chrome circle held two narrow flat ellipses, one stacked on top of the other but each offset to either side, where the outer curve of the ellipse broke through the circle's perimeter. The colliding loops of these described an elongated 'S' shape within the circle. Its plain intention was to suggest an Oriental character. The badge was also seen on the Chairman, a Mercedes-based luxury saloon introduced in 1997. However, it drew ire from Opel: the German company claimed in a German court that it was just too similar to its own emblem.

For two years between 1998 and 2000, SsangYong Motor was owned by Daewoo and its cars were rebadged accordingly, but when that company was declared insolvent SsangYong entered a period of debt-ridden limbo. Nonetheless, it

launched a stylish new off-roader, the Rexton, in 2001, and it was for this experience in the expanding SUV market that SAIC was keen to acquire SsangYong. The Rexton ushered in an all-new logo, too, one that wouldn't annoy Opel: SsangYong has been unable to supply an explanation for it, but it resembles, graphically, a long-feathered bird in the upward-wing position of its flight cycle, while also suggesting the world that the company longs to have in its grasp. Either way, it's used in chrome skeleton as a Rexton bonnet badge and, on the updated Mercedes S Class-based Chairman, as an intriguing-looking bonnet ornament.

STANDARD

Patriotic fervour was long a feature of Standard identity, as seen on the 1938 Standard Flying Eight tourer (opposite) with a Union flag apparently embedded into the top of its radiator grille; but the image changed completely to the 'open book'-style design featured on cars such as the 1948 Vanguard (below).

A British marque that made cars between 1903 and 1963, the 'Standard' name was chosen by company founder Dick Maudslay for its allusion to flag-waving. After the Second World War, following an initial export push, the brand went into decline; US buyers tended to regard 'standard' as the opposite of 'deluxe' – ordinary instead of special – and the name was abandoned in 1963.

Standard cars did not receive a radiator badge until 1908, when a circular brass emblem appeared. The 'STANDARD' word was set on a bar across the centre, while the nucleus of the usually rectangular Union Flag formed the background in red enamel. Later editions added the correct red, white and blue flag colours, while a graphic device fitted to the cars' bumpers featured the flag as its focus with 'STANDARD' above and 'COVENTRY' below it, framed by a Roman legion standard – a piece of battlefield regalia for which, oddly, there is no actual historical record.

In 1931 Standard went with the prevailing car industry fashion and added wings to its logo. The circular centrepiece was mostly as before, with gold-coloured feathers sticking out on either side. Four years later the company introduced its 'Flying Standard' cars, a range with trendy, faux-aerodynamic styling. On these, a Union Flag bonnet ornament was fitted, a three-dimensional object seemingly embedded in the top of the supposedly wind-cheating radiator grille.

The advent of the Standard Vanguard in 1947 brought another change. A new corporate logo had been unveiled in 1945, known in Standard circles as the 'open book'. It was a vaguely shield-inspired trademark: the left-hand 'page' was black, the right one white, while underneath a scroll, upturned at the ends, carried the 'STANDARD CARS' legend. The scroll was split into a white half to the left and a black one at the right to alternate with the 'pages' above. A chrome and black version was fitted to the Vanguard

in 1950, and variations were attached to most subsequent models.

The 1957 Vanguard III Sportsman was a notable anomaly. It boasted a 'globe' badge because it had actually been planned as a Triumph model, Standard having bought this sporty brand in 1945. An unexplained change of heart only weeks before its launch saw the name changed, but it was – presumably – simply too late to alter the badge.

STUDEBAKER

Despite using its original wheel logo and later the 'lazy S' design, Studebaker cars were most notably recognized by their Raymond Loewy-inspired styling, with the propeller nose design (opposite) a memorable high point.

Studebaker is, quite simply, American history: from its origins as a Californian maker of wheelbarrows used in the 'gold rush' of the early nineteenth century to its sad demise as a mass-production car manufacturer in the 1960s – a victim of savage, market-led competition – its aspirations mirrored those of the American nation perfectly.

Brothers Clem and Henry Studebaker, whose family had German roots, turned from making barrows to horsedrawn carts, and their works in South Bend, Indiana had become the world's largest wagon factory by 1871. At one stage it was turning out a vehicle every seven minutes for the US (and even UK) armies. Henry died in 1895, Clem in 1901, so neither witnessed the company's first foray into automobiles with a batch of twenty electric cars. People were impressed, including Thomas Edison who bought one of them, and by 1904 Studebaker offered petrol-powered models too.

Such was the Studebaker reputation for horse-hauled equipment that it didn't stop making such products until 1920. Up to that point, its cars had latterly carried a radiator emblem featuring a cartwheel, with the elaborate 'Studebaker' typescript (the style had originally been a conventional brass pressing attached to the radiator grille mesh) set diagonally across it, bottom left to top right, on a silver sash-like strip. After 1920 the wheel became a car item, complete with wooden spokes and an air valve at the bottom, and surrounded by a white band acting as a visual tyre. From the mid-1930s until the early 1950s they used what Studebaker experts call the 'red ball' logo, with 'STUDEBAKER' in a red circle.

Studebaker cars underwent a styling revolution in 1947 thanks to acclaimed industrial designer Raymond Loewy: 1950 model cars adopted aircraft imagery with a huge chrome propeller motif in the centre of the nose (although this was surmounted by a four-quartered crest in heraldic style as a sop to traditionalists).

Loewy was no stranger to logo design either, having come up with identities for Exxon and Shell, among many others, and he oversaw Studebaker's design update. The basis of this was what one Studebaker fanatic has termed a 'lazy S', a vertical-biased style of the letter flowing fluidly from top to bottom of a circle, backed in a shimmering red on cars, while on paperwork and signage splitting the circle into blue and red halves. It was first seen in the early 1960s.

As each stylish new Studebaker design was rolled out though the 1950s and early 1960s, the consistency of badge design seemed to disintegrate. The one constant tended to be the circular 'S' symbol on hubcaps, but versions of the sporty Hawk coupé also sported their own badge in the form of a rendering of the bird on a thin vertical strip, its raised wing tips almost touching as if descending on its prey. One of the last new Studebakers before the company folded in 1966, the Avanti, carried no badges at all, but was Loewy's most feted automotive design work.

Studebaker de 1950 Coupe de 3 Assentos, Modêlo Champion

Apresentando a última palavra na
nova idade do motorismo . . .

O novo Studebaker de 1950

STUTZ

Stutz made some fine cars, all of which stemmed from a hastily built racing car that nevertheless 'Made Good In A Day' (bottom); from 1926, however, the imagery of the sun god Ra beamed out from the company's cars, radiator mascot and publicity material.

The 1914 Stutz Bearcat is widely regarded as one of America's first classic sports cars. The company's Indiana-based founder, Harry Stutz, built a racing car in just five weeks to prove the worth of his transmission design, with a view to entering it in the very first staging of a local race, the Indianapolis 500 in 1911. Amazingly, it finished eleventh, and he immediately went into production, using the slogan 'The Car That Made Good in a Day'. This made an appearance on his radiator surround badge: across the centre was a pair of dark-blue-enamelled wings with the maker's name spelt out in white as a semi-palindrome, 'STuTZ'. Behind this was a red circle with sun-like beams radiating out from a centre point, while in a white outer band 'THE CAR THAT MADE' was fanned out in the top section above the wings, and 'GOOD IN A DAY' below. Some cars substituted these two half-statements with 'INDIANAPOLIS' and 'INDIANA U.S.A'.

With competition success and the rakish Bearcat, Stutz prospered, and in 1916 sought capital on Wall Street for expansion. Unhappily, by 1919 the financiers had taken control of Stutz, and the founder departed, but a new management in 1922 ushered in a radical redesign of the car in 1926. It now featured a powerful eight-cylinder engine and a low-slung chassis that could accommodate stylish bodies.

For this, a majestic bonnet ornament in the shape of the head of Ra, the ancient Egyptian sun god, was created – the world was still spellbound by the Tutankhamun tomb discovery in 1922. To match it, a new badge was unveiled too. The 'STuTZ' name was as distinctively executed as ever, but the wing feathers had been given a red background resembling sun rays, with a green surround and an intricate blue-and-gold infill pattern at the top.

In 1931 Stutz aimed even higher with a brand new thirty-two-valve, twin-cam engine, together with a revised badge that saw the 'STuTZ' word in black displayed much more clearly on plain white-

enamelled wings. But the economic depression of the times severely suppressed demand, and by 1934 the last of some twenty-five thousand fine Stutz car was built.

SUBARU

Subaru's first car was this Fiat-like 360 model (right, top), but it moved upmarket with the Leone range (right, centre) in 1968, and is now heading for a more European feel with this 2005 concept (right, bottom); the constellation badge, however, as shown opposite on the Impreza, remains a constant.

Subaru's badge is an oval with six four-pointed stars inside it, one large one to the left and five smaller, identically sized ones to the right. In chrome on black, it's been seen on the front of every Subaru car since 1958, when Japan's Fuji Heavy Industries decided to enter the car market. The badge has a special place in the hearts of the Japanese people because it is a representation of the star cluster Pleiades – something that features repeatedly in Japanese culture and literature.

Pleiades is a star cluster in the Taurus constellation. On a clear night its six brightest stars are easily visible to the naked eye; with a telescope, some two hundred and fifty more bluish ones can be seen twinkling. It is mentioned in the eleventh-century Japanese folk story *Makorano-Soshi*, and referred to as 'Matsuraboshi' (six stars) in ancient writings such as *Kojiki* (Record of Ancient Matters). Indeed, *subaru* means 'six stars' in modern-day Japanese, equating to Pleiades, a mythical god named by the ancient

Greeks and whose seven sisters included Maia, Alcyone and Electra.

So much for the historical derivation. In 1954 the car-making side of Fuji built its first prototype and Konji Kita, its president, canvassed his colleagues for name suggestions. When no one could come up with anything appropriate, he went for his own first choice, Subaru. But it had another significance for the company: Fuji Heavy Industries was formed by the merger of six engineering companies, while the word *subaru* has another meaning: to govern or gather together.

A newly adopted signature of recent Subaru concept cars has been a grille design like the air intake of a jet engine, which was intended by chief designer Andreas Zapatinas to summon up Subaru's aerospace heritage in Fuji. The badge, however, remains unchanged.

SUNBEAM-TALBOT

Sunbeam-Talbot was a marque constructed in 1938 by the Rootes Group from two great brands; although enthusiasts derided the move at first, Sunbeam-Talbots excelled in post-war motor sport, as seen opposite on the Monte Carlo Rally.

In 1935 two old-established British marques that were held in very high esteem among enthusiasts were acquired by two people whose *modus operandi* they loathed. The marques were Sunbeam and Talbot; the buyers were William and Reginald Rootes. British car snobs hated them because they had a reputation for buying near-bankrupt car companies and turning them round by making cars with wide public appeal; in the process some wonderful, if totally uneconomic, 'thoroughbred' models were dropped. Sunbeam, for instance, was on the brink mostly because it had spent so much on racing and record-breaking.

Fans were apoplectic in 1938, however, because the ruthless Rootes brothers combined the two makes into a single brand. Even worse, these Sunbeam-Talbots were now simply rebodied versions of Rootes' plebeian Hillmans and Humbers.

Only in the new marque's badge was there any concession to tradition. The Earl of Shrewsbury and Talbot had begun importing French Clement cars in 1903,

and used as his badge the image of the talbot hound, a large hunting dog with long shaggy ears, strong jaws and a terrific nose for tracking when he started building them himself in London. By a happy coincidence, it looked rather like a lion, especially with its tongue outstretched, and the regal imagery was exaggerated by a crown over the dog's head.

Rootes took this majestic picture and added blade-like wings on either side, one reading 'SUNBEAM' and the other 'TALBOT'.

For good measure, they ordered the word 'SUPREME', a Sunbeam model name, to be placed above the crown. To enrage Talbot diehards, the badge was similar in concept to the final Talbot one, which had the words 'TALBOT' and 'LONDON' flanking the main image as two rectangular 'ears'.

By the 1950s, however, the Rootes Group saw the marketing benefit of a ray of light without the canine connotations, and in 1954 the Talbot element was put to sleep when the cars became plain Sunbeams.

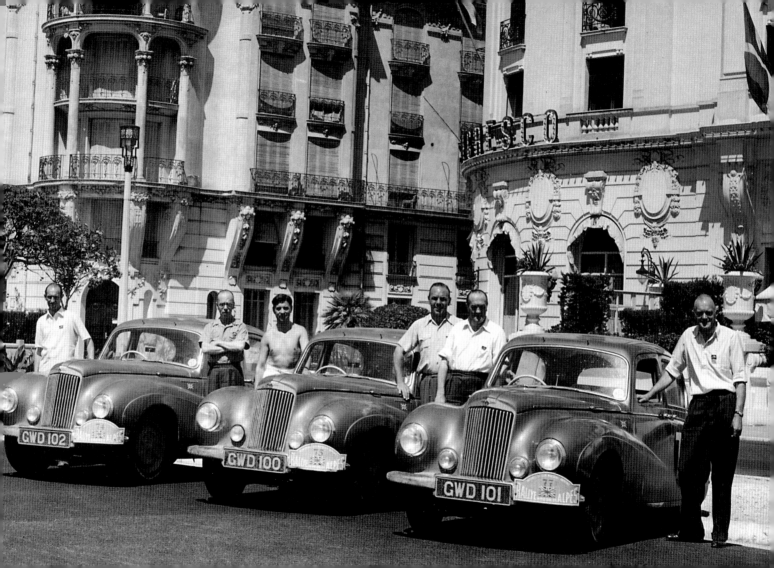

SUZUKI

No hidden message to the Suzuki logo: its three strokes are a simple capital 'S' for Suzuki; the company has a dual speciality in both stylish city cars such as the Swift (opposite) and compact SUVs such as the Vitara (right).

In researching this book, I discovered that many apparently anodyne car badges actually have extremely detailed and interesting stories behind them, none more so than those hailing from Japan. However, I can find nothing extraordinary behind the Suzuki badge, a spiky, compressed rendering of a letter 'S' in three parallel strokes. Even a public relations executive who's been promoting Suzuki cars for two decades could not come up with one scrap of romance or notoriety. "I'd like to be able to embroider it for you, but I can't", he said.

The 'S' stands for Suzuki. And that's it.

The Suzuki Motor Corporation grew out of a family-owned loom-making business. It diversified into motorbikes, launching its first car, the Suzulight, in 1956. Since then, it has specialized in small cars and 4x4 vehicles, and has seen massive growth ever since it reached agreement in 1981 with America's General Motors to sell its cars under various GM brands around the world. Its Alto economy cars,

manufactured in India by Maruti, have also been hugely successful.

Suzuki went through a period of 'badge reticence' in the late 1970s and 1980s, using just a 'SUZUKI' text nameplate, as the symbol was left off the front of the SJ and Swift models. Now, though, it's worn prominently in chrome on a black background on the radiator grille of every model. Unlike Honda, Suzuki uses the same logo on both cars and motorcycles.

Suzuki is one of the most common surnames in the Kanto region, which includes Tokyo. Like all Japanese surnames, it's rooted in nature, the *suzu* element meaning 'bell' and the *ki* part meaning 'tree'. It appears, however, that this particular Suzuki clan decided an 'S' on the front of its cars would work rather better in export markets than representing their products as bell trees…

TALBOT

As a consumer rebranding exercise, Talbot is a textbook failure, although it's easy to say that in retrospect.

In 1978 America's Chrysler sold its entire European division to Peugeot. The price was a symbolic $1 ... plus all Chrysler Europe's debts and liabilities. The deal temporarily made Peugeot, which already owned Citroën, Europe's largest car maker, and it urgently cast around for a new name for its fledgling division. It chose Talbot, a title owned by Chrysler Europe, because it had resonance in both Britain and France, albeit with different pronunciations: Britons said "Tawl-bot" while the French said "Tal-bow". Before 1939 Talbot cars had been built both in London and Paris, the word arising from the complex early involvement of British aristocrat the Earl of Shrewsbury and Talbot.

Peugeot issued various public statements for its new brand, including: "The proud name of Talbot was chosen as being better able to represent this new European role"; and: "We're very proud of our new family name. And so will you be. That's a promise". Dangerous talk.

The new logo consisted of a capital 'T' in a circle in relief. On paper, it appeared stage-lit from top left, the white 'light' casting a blue shadow on raised sections of the 'T' and the circle, while the infill background was in red – a colour scheme designed to have patriotic appeal in both the UK and France. On cars, the emblem was entirely chrome and tended to be mounted against the black plastic of the cars' radiator grilles.

It was a messy transition, with dealers being forced to substitute a plastic 'TALBOT' script for the 'CHRYSLER' one on Sunbeams, Avengers, Horizons and Alpines still in stock, which were nonetheless sold with the old Chrysler radiator badge. By 1980, though, the changeover was complete, and new models such as the 1980 Solara, 1981 Tagora and 1982 Samba followed. Sadly, they were lacklustre cars, and the historical nuances of Talbot were lost on 1980s buyers. In 1985 a new Talbot family car was renamed the Peugeot 309 just prior to launch, signalling an end to the heavily loss-making Talbot venture a year later. In all the car industry takeovers since, no such revival has been attempted.

TATA

A protoype for a Tata sports car (bottom) shows a possible future development for this newly established marque, while the robust Indica and Indigo family cars (opposite and below) has rapidly become the best-selling model on the Indian market.

Any emerging market could do with a character like Ratan Tata, whose determination has seen an all-Indian car brand rise to take on the might of multinational rivals investing in the Indian car industry. It originated unpromisingly as Telco (Tata Locomotive & Engineering Company), a truck and utility vehicle maker that had long been part of his family's Tata conglomerate, founded in the 1860s and involved in everything from steel mills to tea plantations.

Telco's Tata trucks, which had borne the Tata logo for years, were simple, rugged beasts that served their utilitarian duties well. But Mr Tata wanted to expand into cars. In September 1995 he claimed he had a dream that he believed he shared with every Indian dissatisfied with the cars then on offer in India. "We'll have a car with the Zen's size, the Ambassador's internal dimensions, the price of a Maruti 800, and with the running cost of diesel", he declared. In December 1998 the dream was realized in the Indica, a neat five-door

hatchback family car built by Indians with features designed specifically for the home market, particularly a very sturdy body and a 1.4-litre diesel engine.

His hunch was right: by 2001, it had become the fastest-selling automobile in Indian history when it chalked up sales of one hundred thousand in less than eighteen months. It's now into its second incarnation as the V2, with a petrol engine option, and selling faster than ever. Naturally, it wears the Tata corporate logo as a radiator badge. A chrome 'skeleton' ellipse holds a wide letter 'T' in outline, which is derived directly from the corporate symbol usually seen in blue and white.

A deal with Britain's MG Rover Group has seen the Tata Indica enter the European market for the first time under the CityRover name. In July 2003 the division was renamed Tata Motors to reflect its new-found focus; a massive corporate makeover saw the last vestiges of Telco removed from the factory in Pune and from dealers' signage.

TATRA

Built in Czechoslovakia and then the Czech Republic from 1923 until 1998, Tatras were always sturdy, well-engineered machines; the company still makes trucks today. At first they featured a novel backbone-type chassis designed by chief engineer Hans Ledwinka, and in the 1930s the rear-engined Tatra Type 77 and Type 87, with their rear-mounted air-cooled engines, led the world in practical aerodynamic design. The Type 77A was even given a stabilizing fin on its gently sloping rear section to add to its futuristic appearance.

The Tatra name was born in 1923 when the Nesseldorfer company, now liberated from the Austro-Hungarian empire and in newly formed Czechoslovakia, renamed itself Tatra after the biggest mountain in the new nation. A radiator badge took the form of a black-enamelled disc with the white letters of 'TATRA' rising and falling in size to fill the shape; the two crossbars of the 'T's curved to match the circular perimeter exactly.

In 1936 the company was taken over and renamed Ringhoffer-Tatra. The cars routinely carried the red and white Ringhoffer-Tatra corporate logo: the Tatra badge, as before, but doubled in diameter by the addition of a red outer band with 'R-I-N-G-H-O-F-F-E-R' fanned around almost the entire circumference. Then Germany invaded Czechoslovakia in 1938, and the company ultimately found itself nationalized behind the Iron Curtain in 1945.

Post-war Tatras continued the aerodynamic, rear-engined theme, although they dispensed with the backbone chassis. The badge on the 1947 Tatraplan model was the former Tatra logo in rather severe form, coloured red with white letters and with a thin white outer band, with the tops of the 'T's no longer sheltering their fellow letters. The Tatra T2-603 of 1964–75 deployed the badge on a black lozenge-shaped background with a chrome wing sticking out on either side. This big V8-engined car was reserved for Communist Party and embassy officials,

and not sold to the Czech public; perhaps its prominence in diplomatic circles accounted for the legend, in English, 'MADE IN CZECHOSLOVAKIA' curving closely around the underneath of the Tatra logo. The T613-type cars from 1975 until the end returned to the plain Tatra badge, in red on chrome.

TOYOTA

Toyota's early corporate logo (left) used just eight strokes, signifying prosperity, but it was not used on the cars; indeed, Toyotas didn't carry a cohesive marque logo until 1989 when the three-ellipse symbol shown below was unveiled; opposite: the new Toyota Aygo.

Toyota is arguably the most successful car brand of all time, having propelled the company from nowhere to, at one time, the position of world number two car manufacturer. Yet its beginnings were hardly promising.

The wooden textile loom that Sakichi Toyoda perfected in Japan in 1897 was such an extraordinarily efficient piece of machinery that, by 1929, he was able to sell the worldwide patents for it to Britain's Platt Brothers for £100,000 – an emperor's ransom in those days. Not that he retired on the proceeds. Instead, he gave the whole lot to his son Kiichiro Toyoda, so that he could fulfil his dream of making all-Japanese cars. By 1935 he'd built a prototype, and two years later the Model AA was trickling off the production line. Production was low at first as Toyota struggled to get its design and quality absolutely right.

Kiichiro was one of the first car makers to consider what today we call 'brand values'. In July 1937 he held a competition to find a new logo for the firm, which attracted over twenty thousand entries. The winner not only suggested a harmonious shape, in which the Japanese *katakana* characters gave an impression of speed, but because it used only eight brush-strokes for its three characters it was also deemed a symbol of prosperity – eight is a lucky number in Japan, signalling good fortune. The logo was made to match up phonetically with the company name by changing the word from 'Toyoda' to 'Toyota' – which Kiichiro also liked because it distanced the car from its family business roots – and the cars have been called Toyotas ever since.

The original Toyota company logo, however, has never made an appearance on the front or back of one of its cars. Beginning in the 1950s with the Crown, and moving on through the 1960s with the Corona and hugely successful Corolla models, the cars tended to carry individual model livery, just as Fords do. In intricate chrome and plastic radiator

TOYOPET *Crown*

TOYOTA MOTOR

Artwork for a brochure advertising the Toyota Crown (Toyopet was a brand name Toyota abandoned in the 1960s) shows how the company drew inspiration from the Detroit of the late 1950s for its styling.

Toyotas of the 1960s – a
Corolla is shown below, a
Crown sedan bottom –
[t]ended to have
[i]ndividual model liveries
[r]ather than a strong
[m]arque identity,
[f]ollowing the Ford and
Chrysler approach of
[n]o-logo design at that
[ti]me.

medallions, there was, rather obviously, a crown symbol for the Crown, while the Corolla carried a capital 'C' topped with three small five-pointed stars. The badges looked a bit tacky, but buyers loved the cars' reliability.

Many Toyotas, including the Land Cruiser 4x4 off-roader, simply made do with the word 'TOYOTA' spelt out in large plain letters; beginning in 1978 and with the launch of the Toyota Starlet economy car, Toyota cleaned up its badge act by applying this policy across the board. Nevertheless, it was hardly a badge as such – more a textual statement.

In 1989, however, Toyota decided to unite its corporate image and its cars' badges with an all-new logo consisting of three ellipses. The ellipse shape was selected, the company said, because it contained two central points, one representing the heart of its customers and the other the heart of its products. Two of the ellipses bisected one another to form a 'T', standing for Toyota, while an outer one

encircled an empty background, suggesting the limitless opportunities available to the company. Any similarity to a man wearing a Stetson hat staring through an oval window was wrong, if mildly amusing.

In the fifteen years since, the logo has been applied with reasonable consistency, only some Japanese home market cars such as the Mark II and Century sticking with a bewildering medley of individual model badges. Most Toyotas, and all models for sale outside Japan, carry the logo as a chrome cut-out attached to either black or silver plastic grilles or else bolted to the metalwork of the nose, with the paint colour showing through as the background infill colour. On corporate communications it is shown in red outline.

TRABANT

Bizarrely, the 1958–91 Trabant was characterized by a badge featuring a bold capital 'S', but then the East German manufacturer didn't have to worry too much about marketing – there was usually a waiting list even for this mediocre car.

The collapse of the Berlin Wall in 1989 was the most symbolic event in the ending of the Cold War between East and West. But the emergence of the Trabant, spluttering its way into a bright new Europe, was the automotive equivalent.

West German motorists were horrified at the highly polluting two-stroke 600 cc engine in the car, its rudimentary safety systems and its body made from a type of resin-strengthened wood pulp and cotton. But that is what East German drivers had had to put up with since November 1957, when the first 'Trabbi' was introduced as just about the only small car the country's citizens could realistically hope to get hold of.

Weirdly, for a car officially known as the Trabant P601, a circular outline bonnet badge carried a prominent 'S' scrawled diagonally (bottom left to top right) across it in pseudo-streamlined style as its only feature. It was a legacy of the East German government's policy of nationalization. After the eastern part of the country was

annexed in 1945, the former Audi and Horch factories found themselves locked behind the Iron Curtain, and in 1958 the East German authorities forced them to merge to form VEB Sachsenring Automobilwerke. Sachsenring was the name of a racing circuit, as well as a large saloon car built by Horch for government officials; it now became the inspiration for the 'S' on the Trabant.

It was initially affixed to the Trabant's radiator grille, and seen in silver on a black circle with an elegant, tapering chrome fin jutting out on either side, but by the 1970s this had become a chrome bonnet badge, and when the last cars were made in 1991 it had turned into a black plastic fixture.

TRIUMPH

The two versions of the Triumph 'world' badge (left) indicated a change in attitude to the British empire, while the 'open book' badge later became a fixture on cars such as the TR3 (opposite); the final Triumph sports car, the TR7 (below) took the straightforward 'laurels' approach.

Triumph cars were launched by the motorbike company in 1923. They were given a completely new logo strongly redolent of the dying days of the British empire. A gently domed, circular enamelled badge had a map of the world as a background. The landmass was multicoloured, but the British 'possessions' were shown in red, the sea of course being blue. The map was vaguely drawn, bizarrely using the Indian subcontinent as its focal point, with the UK shown at the edge of the circle on the top left. Chrome lines of latitude and longitude crisscrossed it, and across the centre was 'TRIUMPH' in white, orbiting the globe.

The car and motorbike divisions split in 1936, and shortly after this Triumph toned down the imperial nature of its badge by making all the land on it red. 'Triumph' was now depicted as if handwritten, the stem of the 'r' curling round to underscore the word.

Triumph cars continued to use this badge until 1953, when the TR2 sports car

went on sale. Triumph was now owned by the Standard Motor Company and adapted its 'open book' corporate logo into a new badge. It was a rather unattractive chrome shield, the central part of which displayed ribs in the form of vertical, black-enamelled bands, while a scroll across the bottom and curling round the ends carried the word 'TRIUMPH'; 'TR' and '2' were stacked on a chrome plinth at the top. On later models such as the TR4 and Herald, the badge did without its text and featured contrasting black and white enamelled 'quarters', while the word 'T-R-I-U-M-P-H' was spelt out in separate chrome letters fixed straight on to the bodywork.

This badge also vanished in 1966, when 'TRIUMPH' became merely an anonymous oblong nameplate usually bolted to the right-hand side of the cars' fronts. In 1979, however, a distinctive Triumph identity was resumed in the form of a large black circular decal on the nose section of the TR7 sports car. 'TRIUMPH' was augmented by a semicircular garland above and

below, presumably to signify success in motor sport. Slightly incongruously, this image was transferred to a four-sided plastic badge with a silver design on a black background in 1981 for the last Triumph of all, the Acclaim. A licence-built version of Honda's Ballade saloon, the Acclaim was the first Japanese-designed car built in the UK; production ended in 1984.

Triumph T.R.3 Sports

TVR

The animalistic TVR Sagaris (opposite) is worlds away from the company's roots in Trevor Wilkinson's backstreet garage in Blackpool, England; still, the consonants in the founder's name survive in the badge. Below: the M series cars of the 1970s were the bedrock for the success of today's marque, now under Russian ownership.

TVR is shorthand for 'Trevor', the first name of the founder of the sports car company based in Blackpool, England. A TVR today, such as the Tuscan, Tamora or Sagaris, is a reward that many successful young British men give themselves – a growling two-seater sports car. Trevor Wilkinson, by contrast, left school in Blackpool in 1937 aged fourteen with not a qualification to his, as yet, unremarkable name. However, he was apprenticed with a local garage before setting up his own workshop called Trevcar Motors. In 1947 Wilkinson built himself a sports car from the remains of an old Alvis, and a year later he renamed his company TVR Engineering.

His big break came in 1956 when an American car fanatic asked him to produce a 'backbone'-type chassis for US sports car racing. This prototype led to the TVR Grantura production car in 1958. It may have been crude but it was a rapid machine and, because it used parts from other cars, was sold at affordable prices. It had a simple chrome outline badge: a coin-sized oval tightly encircled the 'TVR' letters, the 'V' bursting out of the bottom to form a short 'stalk'. Slightly longer horizontal bars jutted out on both sides, while two parallel strips across the top, seemingly sprouting from the ends of the two stems of the 'V', formed wings that tapered to unswept tips.

By mid-1960 Wilkinson had sold his hundredth car, but two years later he sold up and had nothing else to do with the car that carried his name. Shortly afterwards, the basic TVR logo still used today made its debut, the three letters on a dark-green rectangle (later changed to blue) with the horizontal stroke of the 'T' forming a line that turns into the 'V', the right-hand stem of which is also the stem of the 'R'. Beneath this was proudly stated 'ENGLAND'.

TVR's glory days followed, with the TVR Griffith of the 1960s, the M series in the 1970s and the Tasmin/350i of the 1980s. The 1980 Tasmin initially brought a new badge, the 'TVR' letters displayed as a large decal on the wedge-shaped nose, struck through

with horizontal lines showing the contrasting body colour underneath.

In 1986 TVR revived its stubby, buxom shape of old with the S roadster, and the decal gave way to a metal cut-out of the by now widely recognized 'TVR' lettering, enamelled in several colours, including purple, with chrome showing through between the horizontal lines of colour. It is still in use today, as is another bonnet decal-type badge in an oval shape but still holding the familiar 'TVR' text style.

VAUXHALL

The circular badge on cars manufactured and sold by Vauxhall – General Motors' exclusively British brand name – has a chromed metal surround, a black background and a silver design. It shows a griffin, an imaginary animal consisting of a lion's body with an eagle's head, beak and wings, which is depicted rearing up on its hind legs while holding a flag with its two claws. On the end of the staff, curved to fit in the circle, is a flag with the letter 'V' on it. This emblem is a survivor from Vauxhall's existence before 1925, the year it was acquired by GM in its first step to becoming a global company. However, Vauxhall's griffin isn't quite as old as many people think.

Until the First World War the cars carried the 'VAUXHALL' name on a simple brass plate bolted to the radiator shell, and latterly a circular 'VM' (for Vauxhall Motors) monogram. In 1915 works manager Laurence Pomeroy decided this wasn't good enough, and offered a prize of two guineas to any employee who could devise something better. His only stipulations were that it must have historic or artistic merit.

A young engineer called Harry Varley responded to this challenge. Varley went to the library in Luton, the Bedfordshire town where Vauxhall's factory was based, and discovered the crest of one Fulk le Breant, a mercenary from Normandy whose services were much in demand from King John (1166–1216). He prospered in the king's court, becoming the sheriff of Oxford and Hertford and also being granted the manor of Luton for his sometimes grisly services. Fulk le Breant then married Margaret de Redvers, whose hand came with a substantial home on the south bank of the River Thames in London, close to where the MI6 headquarters building is now. The house was soon known as Fulk's Hall, through time corrupted to Fawkes Hall, Foxhall and ultimately to Vauxhall – the name of the surrounding area in London's Lambeth borough to this day.

By an incredible coincidence, this was

where a Scottish engineer called Alexander Wilson established the Vauxhall Iron Works in 1857 to make engines for paddle steamers. His company entered the car industry in 1903. Just two years later its directors decided to relocate Vauxhall Motors to Luton, where the Fulk le Breant association had existed since the thirteenth century.

So Harry Varley carefully drew a freehand interpretation of the crest and submitted it for the badge contest. He was declared the winner, on one condition: Pomeroy said the idea was good but the drawing poor. Afraid of breaching copyright rules, Varley was unwilling to copy it too closely but, faced with Pomeroy's threat to withdraw the prize, he faithfully traced the crest, complete with the griffin's head turned to look over its leonine shoulder, and got his money. A prototype was made with the griffin in gold on a blue background, and a black band around the edge carrying the words 'VAUXHALL • MOTORS LTD • LONDON'. Why

it said London and not Luton is unclear; it was changed to 'LUTON, ENGLAND' on production cars.

The emblem became more ovular in the 1940s but was circular once more for the 1954–58 era Vauxhall Velox and Cresta, albeit with the 'LUTON' word removed. Thereafter, as for many marques during the 1960s, 'VAUXHALL' text nameplates mostly replaced badges until the 1972 Victor FE. Starting with this car, the griffin gained a trendy makeover, redesigned as either a chrome edged, red-painted casting or else as an emblem with a square frame; on 1980s cars it was a silvered plastic moulding.

The 1986 Vauxhall Carlton ushered in a return to a circular form, while the 1995 Vectra carried the badge as used today, with a bolder, smoother griffin image nestling inside the point of a large chrome 'V' incorporated into the grille design.

VOLGA

Volga's GAZ-24 model (shown opposite) remains Russia's staple workhorse as taxi, police car and business transport – but is very rarely exported; below: the leaping stag has been on every Volga, including the venerable GAZ-21 (bottom).

This is a tricky one to categorize, as the factory and marque is called GAZ, standing for the Gorkovsky Avtomobilny Zavod (or Gorky Auto Plant), near the city of Nizhny Novgorod (formerly called Gorky), but the cars that it is famous for are called Volgas, and have been sold under the Volga marque name whenever vain attempts have been made to market them outside former Soviet bloc regions.

Every Volga since the first in 1956 has been a tough, rugged machine. Then, just as now, they carried a red shield badge with a silver leaping stag in the centre to demonstrate that mechanical brawn, with the three Russian characters equating to GAZ underneath. It's very similar to the design on postage stamps for the Gorky area. Today's cars, such as the popular 3102 saloon, carry the emblem in the centre of a pugnaciously slatted chrome grille. Early cars underscored the badge with a flattened 'V'-shaped decoration, while later ones had a triangular plinth.

According to Julian Nowill, an expert in cars from Eastern Europe and Russia, firms such as GAZ "have never had much imagination when it comes to model names". The Volga car gets its name from the river on which the GAZ factory stands.

GAZ specializes in trucks and vans; indeed, its first products were licence-built Ford AA pick-ups. Its Volga cars are old-fashioned machines used all over Russia as taxis and for other dutiful roles. The first Volga model, the type GAZ-21, was replaced by the type GAZ-24 in 1968. Incredibly, all of today's Volga car range is still based on this latter model, albeit with numerous modifications, and its bulletproof nature means that it still finds a ready market – in 2002 over eighty thousand Volgas were sold, making it Russia's second best-selling car brand. Other cars that this Russian giant has built include the Pobeida (meaning 'victory') in the 1940s and the Chaika (the name of a gull-like bird that breeds on the nearby Volga river) limousine for diplomats and Soviet officials from the 1950s to the 1980s.

VOLKSWAGEN

October 1948 witnessed a small milestone in Volkswagen history: the company's logo, a 'V' sitting on top of the centre point of a 'W' and enclosed in a circle, was officially registered as a trademark. The origins of this design are obscure, however. A template for a *Volks wagen*, or 'people's car', was drawn up by Dr Ferdinand Porsche in 1934 for the Nazi government. Volkswagenwerk GmbH was formed in 1937, and construction of the Wolfsburg factory began a year later; the symbol must have been designed simultaneously, as photographs show it on a Volkswagen training centre building at Brunswick, which opened in 1938.

All early Beetle production after the Second World War was reserved for the Allied forces, and bore no badges at all, but in 1949 an 'Export' model was announced, and shortly afterwards cars left the plant with two bonnet badges. At the back of the bonnet's peaked centre line, just below the windscreen, the 'VW' roundel was bolted on as a three-

dimensional chrome badge, facing skywards, while an enamelled shield was fitted at the front of the bonnet.

The new town of Wolfsburg in Lower Saxony had been built around the giant Volkswagen factory, and named after the nearby Wolf's Castle, built in 1451. The badge reflected Wolfsburg's civic crest, freshly created in 1945. A grey castle with an open city gate was at the centre, fronted by two wavy blue lines representing the nearby Aller river. Between the castle's twin turrets, a red wolf glared back at its own aggressively erect tail.

Volkswagen began making cars in Brazil in 1953, and the Wolfsburg crest soon faded from prominence, being totally supplanted in 1962 by the 'VW' symbol, which survives to this day on every modern Volkswagen. The 1950 Transporter van featured an enormous painted 'VW' emblem as the centrepiece of its frontal design, endearing it to millions. Today's Volkswagens, from the Polo to the Touareg, carry the symbol in chrome as one of the

largest, clearest badges on the front of any new cars. However, the Wolfsburg insignia remained on Volkswagens such as the Passat and Golf into the late 1970s, usually moulded into the plastic steering wheel centre.

Volkswagen badges have been the subject of two crime waves. In 1957–58 over a million of the Wolfsburg crests were stolen from Volkswagen Beetles in the USA, beginning in New York and spreading to the West Coast; as the replacement cost was $3.05 apiece, it represented a three-million-dollar theft. Professor Müller of New York University's Law School conducted a criminological investigation into the "crest larceny" phenomenon, and discovered that the culprits were thirteen- and fourteen-year-old boys who prised them off with penknives. If they were prepubescent, they kept the badge, sometimes wearing it as a belt buckle; if puberty had begun, they gave them to girlfriends as keepsakes.

In the UK in 1986–87, thousands of the

A festival of Volkswagen badges including (below) the latest Mk5 Golf, the logo formed a major design centrepiece on the original Volkswagen Kombi in 1950 (opposite, top right), being even larger than the van's headlights.

round 'VW' badges were stolen by teenagers, who wore them on neck chains to emulate the white rap group The Beastie Boys. Volkswagen had an unspoken policy of offering free replacements to distraught owners, while Beastie Boys fans were offered VW keyrings if they stopped stealing the emblems.

VOLVO

Modern Volvos come with a vertically slatted grille divided by a bar that runs diagonally from a quarter of the way along the bottom to three-quarters of the way along the top. Exactly in the centre of the grille, the bar passes behind a square black badge, edged in chrome. Across the centre of the badge is 'VOLVO' in silver on an oblong strip, coloured dark-blue, and this itself straddles a silver circle with, at its top right-hand corner, an arrow pointing diagonally towards the continuation of the bar. The effect is to draw the eye across the front of the car, emphasizing its size.

The circle with its arrow is the mapping symbol for iron (and also the sign for the planet Mars). It was chosen to express the intentions of the founders and backers of Volvo: to build a high-quality car (from Swedish steel) that was also sturdy enough to cope with Sweden's often tortuous roads. Its appearance on Volvos has been consistent since the inception of the Volvo marque in 1927. Indeed, the first car, called the Jakob, had its radiator mesh fronted by a diagonal bar with the symbol in the centre, just like today. In those days, there was also a radiator badge, which comprised an underlined 'VOLVO' in white, Egyptian-style, heavy-serif letters on a blue oval background with a white banner below saying 'GOTHENBURG SWEDEN', but even this typography is similar to the one used by Volvo today. The Jakob's stylist, Helmer Olsson, oversaw the design.

There have been some variations in the intervening seventy-plus years. For example, it was absent altogether from Volvo cars between 1944 and 1958, when it was reinstated on all models of the PV544; earlier PV444/544 cars of the 1940s and 1950s made do with a small chrome 'V' on the front of the bonnet lid. The 1960 P1800 sports coupé had the symbol in black enamel on a chrome, three-sided shield on its low-slung nose, while the 164 3-litre luxury saloon of 1968 featured the badge in the top right-hand corner of the grille, and the welcome return of the diagonal bar. The current badge dates from 1998.

WOLSELEY

Britain's Wolseley marque isn't remembered these days for anything much, but in badge terms the company has one major innovation to its fusty name: it was the first and, so far, only marque in the world to feature an illuminated badge. True, America's obscure Fageol 100 of 1916 also had one, carved from ivory and lit up when the headlights were on, but only prototypes were ever made; Wolseley, by comparison, gave every model in its range a glowing radiator badge in 1932. Owners christened it the 'ghost light'.

Before that (the cars were first built in 1900, and in 1927 the company was taken over by Morris), the Wolseley badge had been neat, if plain, elliptical in shape and garlanded at its metal edge. On a cream background, the word 'WOLSELEY' was spelt out in blue with a line underscoring it, and was notable principally for a 'W' in the unmistakable shape of a lyre.

When it was turned into a light in 1932, enamel gave way to an oval of thin opaque cream Bakelite, and later plastic.

A tiny bulb was automatically switched on with the headlights, giving a warm glow behind the 'WOLSELEY' name in crimson. This was useful to speeding drivers in the late 1930s because Wolseleys were widely used by police forces across England – if you saw the badge in your rear-view mirror, it was time to behave!

It proved a handy marketing tool for the cars, too. After the Second World War, Wolseleys were pretty much identical to Morris and other BMC cars, differentiated only by so-called 'badge engineering'. Inevitably, this led to a loss of character; sales slowed until the last Wolseley, still with its illuminated badge, was sold in 1976. Today, mention of Wolseley is likely to mean The Wolseley, an acclaimed restaurant in Piccadilly, London, housed in what was originally Wolseley's own showroom.

ZAGATO

Zagato is one of a select group of Italian design bureaux. Along with Bertone, Italdesign and Pininfarina, it has never engineered its own cars from scratch, but has provided striking bodywork designs for other manufacturers' chassis – both on a one-off, bespoke basis and in series. The company, founded by craftsman Ugo Zagato in 1919, has been responsible for more than two hundred car designs.

Carrozzeria Zagato was once a coachbuilder like Bertone and Pininfarina, but the difficulty in finding contracts large enough to keep its Milan factory operating drove it to the brink of bankruptcy in 1993. With the plant now in mothballs, it is today purely a design consultancy. Its latest car design work can be seen in the limited-edition Zagato versions of the Aston Martin DB7, although visitors to Milan can also travel in a very different Zagato-designed vehicle – the sleek new Eurotram, which won the 2002 Compasso d'Oro, Italy's most coveted industrial design trophy.

The DB7, of course, has an Aston Martin badge on its nose but a Zagato badge on its front wing, between the front wheel arch and the door opening. In common with most Zagato-bodied cars since the early 1950s, this is a 'Z' with an upturned serif on the left-hand end of the top crossbar, and a down-turned one at the right-hand end of the bottom one. On the top bar 'ZAGATO' is engraved, on the bottom one 'MILANO'.

On Zagato's exquisitely designed two-seater sports car bodies for pre-war Alfa Romeo chassis, the company's name was displayed on a rectangular metal nameplate on the bottom of the doors. In the 1950s, however, Zagato designers often specified two-tone paintwork on the aero-dynamic bodies that the company built, with a zigzag colour-split suggesting the letter 'Z'. This treatment didn't suit every design, so the now-familiar 'Z' badge was created. It was enamelled in black with silver text on the many lightweight sporting bodies that Zagato produced on chassis by Alfa Romeo, Lancia, Aston Martin and Fiat-Abarth; today it is brushed aluminium.

ZHONGHUA

The handsome ZhongHua saloon has, besides its other merits, a unique distinction: on 16 December 2000 it became the first world-class passenger car to be launched with intellectual property rights fully under Chinese control. It was built by the Shenyang Gold-Cup Auto-Making Company in north-east China's Liaoning province, which is owned by Shanghai-based China Brilliance Automotive Holdings, and went on full sale across the country in 2002.

This was a tremendously important step for China. Until then, and even now with the vast majority of other vehicles made in the country, cars have been either licence-built from foreign companies or based on foreign designs, especially from Japan and the USA. So no wonder the ZhongHua sports a distinctive bonnet badge – a chrome circle – with the Chinese character for Zhong inside it. Zhong means China, while ZhongHua means all of China.

China Brilliance has various joint ventures, including one with BMW, but the ZhongHua is all its own work. Well, almost. The company sought the help of several European consultancies in its $500 million project to design the 2-litre executive saloon. The styling is by Italy's Giorgetto Giugiaro, Mitsubishi provided the 2- and 2.4-litre engines, BMW helped with engineering, while Britain's MIRA conducted performance, climatic and safety testing in the UK and on the high-altitude roads of Tibet. At least four German firms were consulted on manufacturing techniques. This is an impressive pedigree for a total newcomer.

The company admits that the car is tailored to Chinese tastes, particularly in its chrome-laden styling, and so far it has not been exported to 'mature' markets. But its replacement is sure to be chasing world sales, so that Zhong symbol could soon be joining those of Toyota, Chevrolet and Volkswagen on a highway near you.

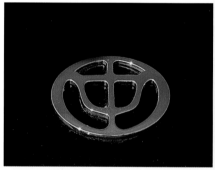

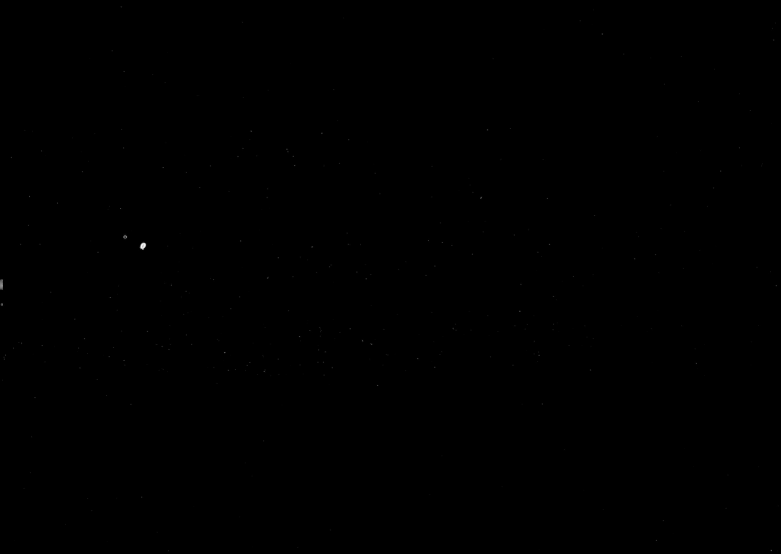

PICTURE CREDITS

ACKNOWLEDGEMENTS

Researching this book, and endeavouring to make its contents as accurate as possible, would have been utterly impossible without the kind help and generosity of these people:

Giulietta Calabrese at Fiat UK; Alan Stote at Red Triangle; Barbara Prince at Aston Martin Lagonda; Robin Davies at Audi UK; David Whyley, Austin historian; Duncan Forrester at BMW GB; Richard Day, curator of The Bugatti Trust; Hannah Burgess at PFPR Communications on behalf of Cadillac Europe; Ian Adcock, a journalist colleague with extensive knowledge of the Chinese car industry; Xuan Lin at the Chinese Trade Delegation in London; Barry Dressel, manager of the Walter P Chrysler Museum; John Reynolds, Citroen historian; Denis Chick at GM Daewoo and now Chevrolet; Leslie Armbruster, Research Services Archivist, Ford Motor Company; Arthur Fairley & Anne Nash at IM Group; Karen Eliatamby and staff, Embassy of Japan, London; Anders Clausager & John Maries,

Jaguar Daimler Heritage Trust; Peter Jacobs, Delage Section of the Vintage Sports Car Club; Barry Collins, Coventry Transport Museum; Peggy Vezina at the General Motors Media Archive; Lawrence Pearce at Honda UK; Rodney Kumar at Hyundai Cars; Wayne Bruce at Nissan Motor GB; David Windsor at PFPR; Simon Rosenkranz, Invicta enthusiast; Keith Anderson, Jensen historian; Karin Schlesiger & Soonjung Kwon at Willhelm Karmann; Arnold Davey, The Lagonda Club; Kelly Burton at RSM, for Lamborghini information; Chris Clark, author of The Lanchester Legacy; Lisa Watts at Land Rover; Alun Parry & Caroline James at Lexus GB; Jane Knibbs at DaimlerChrysler; Gabi Whitfield at Mitsubishi Motors; Jon Pressnell, Morris expert; John Bath, Packard Automotive Club; Sophie Stephenson, Perodua UK; Bernard J Weis & Arnold Romberg, Pierce-Arrow Society; John Hall, Riley enthusiast; Roger Mercer at RM Communications; Ian Rimmer, Peter Baines & Malcolm Tucker, Rolls-Royce Enthusiasts'

Club; Gary Axon at Saab Great Britain; Juliet Edwards at Seat GB; Andy Kirk, representing Shelby; Katerina Svejdarova at Skoda UK; Debbie Hull at smart; John Heffernan, design consultant to SsangYong; Professor Ken Greenley, creative director of SsangYong Motors; The Standard Motor Club; Andrew Beckman, archivist at the Studebaker Museum; David Farquhar at Suzuki GB; Julian Nowill, expert in Eastern European cars and a member of the Unloved Soviet Socialist Register; Richard Sails, archivist of the TVR Car Club; David Burgess-Wise, motoring historian and chronicler of Vauxhall's centenary; Dmitri Pronin & Vladimir Varaksin, both Moscow-based enthusiasts for Volga (and Chaika) cars; Paul Buckett at Volkswagen Group UK; Dr Ulrike Gutzmann & Dr Manfred Grieger at the Corporate History Department, Volkswagen AG; John Lefley at Volvo Car UK; Joanne Marshall, author and Zagato historian; Tim Olley, a renowned collector of car badges, who scanned the manuscript for obvious errors, and thankfully found few.

First Published 2005 by
Merrell Publishers Limited
www.merrellpublishers.com

Head office
81 Southwark Street
London SE1 0HX

New York office
49 West 24th Street, 8th Floor
New York, NY 10010

Text © Giles Chapman 2005
www.gileschapman.com
Design & layout © Merrell Publishers
Limited 2005
Illustrations © the copyright holders

Publisher Hugh Merrell
Editorial Director Julian Honer
US Director Joan Brookbank
Sales and Marketing Director
Kim Cope
Sales and Marketing Assistant
Nora Kamprath
Managing Editor Anthea Snow
Junior Editor Helen Miles
Art Director Nicola Bailey
Junior Designer Paul Shinn
Production Manager Michelle Draycott
Production Controller Sadie Butler

British Library Cataloguing-
in-Publication Data: Chapman, Giles
Car badges : the ultimate guide to
automotive logos worldwide

1.Automobiles - Trademarks
2.Automobiles - Radiator ornaments
3.Logos (Symbols)
I.Title 629.2'22'0277

ISBN: 1 85894 275 6

Produced by Merrell Publishers
Designed by Untitled
Picture Research by Helen Stallion
Copy-edited by Kim Richardson

Printed and bound in Singapore